THE
POACHER'S COOKBOOK

THE POACHER'S COOKBOOK

Game and Country Recipes

PRUE COATS

wood engravings by

BARBARA GREG

White Lion Books

CAMBRIDGE

White Lion Books
44 High Street
Balsham
Cambridge CB1 6EP
Tel (0223) 893632 Fax (0223) 894703

First published in 1993 by White Lion Books

ISBN 1 874 762 05 8

British Library Cataloguing-in-Publication-Data
A catalogue record for this book is available from the
British Library

The publishers are grateful to Marian and Michael Janes for their
help in lending some of Barbara Greg's wood engravings and for their support

Designed by Clare Byatt

Typeset in 11pt Garamond by
Solutions for Business.

Printed by Biddles Ltd, England

THIS BOOK IS DEDICATED
with love, to
GLAD, JENNY, MICK and MIKE

ACKNOWLEDGEMENTS

Firstly, the most important person to thank is Ian Niall for approving of me as a fit person to write the companion book to his classic *The Poacher's Handbook*. I was most honoured to be asked. Likewise, Marian and Michael Janes for the use of Barbara Greg's wonderfully evocative wood engravings, many of which have appeared in early editions of Ian Niall's books, to illustrate my book. I should also like to thank the following for their invaluable help, advice and ideas: my friendly publishing team, Deirdre and Michael Hyde and Linda and Robert Yeatman for all their hard work and enthusiasm; Sue Ross for her meticulous editing; Sue Ferguson for undertaking to read and correct my recipes; Lucy, my daughter, for her professional advice, recipes and suggestions and Richard her husband, for his 'Piggy Pudding' comments; Susan Askew for so kindly giving me her mother's and grandmother's recipes; Kenneth McLellan for the tale of the traditional grouse harvest; Mrs Watkins, Katie, Mary, Carole, Jonathan Young, Anthony, George Parker, Mike Swan, John Soper, Inige and Eva and all my dear friends who so unselfishly parted with their cherished recipes; the Gamekeeper's Inn, Mapledurwell for their help with the Rook Pie. Especial thanks to David Fleet for producing the squirrels for me to cook, Glad, without whose support this book would never have been written, Jenny, Mick and Mike for so patiently tasting and evaluating and for their opinion and help; also to Guy Garfit and Alex Slater of Solutions for Business and Clare Byatt for their invaluable help in transforming these recipes into an elegant book. My grateful thanks to the Editors of *The Field, Shooting Times and Country Magazine* and *Countrysport* for allowing me to use extracts from my articles in their magazines.

PRUE COATS
Dummer 1993

CONTENTS

INTRODUCTION

I was most flattered when I was asked to write *The Poacher's Cookbook* as a companion volume to Ian Niall's inimitable classic *The Poacher's Handbook* and I have thoroughly enjoyed doing so. My personal knowledge of poaching is limited to an episode when I was twelve years old on Exmoor, but with my late husband Archie's (and my) involvement with gamekeepers I have, over the years, amassed a fair number of anecdotes, some of which I have recounted in the appropriate sections of this book.

We all have in our mind's eye the archetypal gypsy/poacher sitting outside his caravan, horse hobbled nearby, and a fire of twigs and fallen branches with the big black pot simmering away on its tripod. Some still survive but they are few and far between, unlike the pre-war years when many houses and farms sported a notice saying, 'No HAWKERS, GYPSIES OR TINKERS. BEWARE THE DOG.' As for the rest, modern times have caught up with them and they live in motor caravans on sites and if they poach it is as an intimidating rabble with packs of lurchers.

No romance alas either, for the other kind of poacher described by Ian Niall. Nowadays they work in gangs and are armed with firearms which they do not hesitate to use, making the keeper's life a dangerous one. Others use dynamite in rivers to achieve their aim, but as long as we have *The Poacher's Handbook* we can see how it once was, and that there was indeed some romance to poaching.

The poachers of whom Ian Niall writes were poor country folk who either ate their ill-gotten gains, or sold them to feed their families. My daughter Lucy's old nanny, Frankie, left school at twelve and went out to work for 1/- (5p) a week. When she married, she brought up four children on £2 a week, so thrift was second nature and nothing was wasted. Meat was a luxury and her husband's lunchbox consisted of bread and dripping and a bottle of cold tea. When there was no work to be had he

walked forty miles to Wiltshire to pull turnips. As he slept
rough, no doubt some of the turnips found their way into the
pot with, I suspect, the odd rabbit.

I was brought up during World War II when the motto was
'make do and mend', so I too cannot bear to waste anything.
Some people seem to think there is a kind of stigma attached to
the word 'left-overs' but I call it 'progressive cookery' as you can
often devise a dish, planning ahead what you will do with it
afterwards.

Country cookery before the war was pretty stodgy and contained a lot of lard, as most villagers kept a pig. Food in grand
houses was over-rich, a legacy from Victorian and Edwardian
times. Now the pendulum has swung the other way to *nouvelle
cuisine*. I am not a fashionable cook, my only dictum is that it
should taste good and the flavours enhance one another. Game,
in all its variety, is healthy and full of taste. The only reason
some of the dishes may appear somewhat rich is that there is
often little fat content in the meat, so butter, oil, cream or wine
have to be used to tenderise and make it more succulent. Some
of my recipes come from abroad and to prove that poaching is
not the prerogative of the British, I have included the *furtivo* of
Spain and the French *braconnier*.

Game lends itself particularly to robust country dishes, many
of which can be found in a slightly different guise in the peasant
cookery of other lands, the variations deriving from the available
local produce, one example being the olives which are so often
included in the casseroles of Provence.

I have tried to give as varied a selection of recipes as possible, from down-to-earth stomach-fillers to slightly more *nouvelle cuisine* recipes. I hope you will find something to your taste. I hasten to add that you don't need to take up poaching to get your game - most large supermarkets sell it and if they don't have what you want, try and suss out your local game dealer.

Nevertheless, many of the recipes in this book contain ingredients which are only to be found in the country and so I have tried to give alternatives that are readily available in supermarkets. One of my main cooking tenets is, if you haven't got it, try something else. You never know, you may even have made the culinary discovery of a lifetime, so use your imagination!

Capable cooks may wonder at the length of some of my cooking times, but having been in the game business for forty-odd years I have had to deal with a variety of species, both young and old. In my experience, particularly where pigeons are concerned, you either cook them very fast over a high heat as for steak or long and slow as though tenderising a cheap cut of meat. The same goes for hare and venison. It is impossible to tell what age the game is that you buy from supermarkets so it is best to err on the conservative side with your cooking times. If your game is freshly shot it is likely to be young, but with pheasants watch out for the old stager with long spurs. He will be best casseroled, or made into a pie or soup.

Where recipes mention a food processor or blender it does not mean that you cannot make them without these. Chopping, mincing or in the case of purées, sieving or passing through a *mouli-legumes* will do just as well. If you cannot afford a food processor or do not have space in a small kitchen, the next best thing is one of those hand held electric chopper/blenders of which there are several varieties on the market. I was given one for Christmas and did not imagine that I would ever use it as I have a very good food processor, but for soups, purées and mashing vegetables I would not now be without it. For game cookery a filleting/boning knife, cook's knife and small knife are essential plus the means to keep them very sharp. If you cannot cope with a steel, a sharpening stone, 'Chantry' pull through sharpener or electric sharpener will do as well.

The recipes are grouped under the different species of game, beginning with feather, moving on through fur to fish. Between feather and fur there is a section on Mixed Game for those occasions in the shooting season, or when you are clearing out the deep freeze, when you may want to combine several different kinds of game in one recipe.

At the end of each section I have included some recipes for puddings, drinks, jellies and other country foods, choosing seasonal produce what I hope is an appropriate taste to go with that game or fish. But I offer no hard and fast suggestions - do browse through the different sections and choose the puddings and other side-dishes and drinks that appeal to you.

At the end of the book is a collecton of basic methods that recur frequently in the recipes in this book. This avoids long and unwieldy descriptions in the individual recipes and is mainly for those who are not quite such experienced cooks.

PHEASANT

My two favourite poaching stories involve pheasants. The first concerns a very cheeky poacher who was the bane of all the local game keepers. He would ring up and issue a challenge, saying that he was going to 'do' such and such a wood on a certain night and no matter what precautions they took he invariably got away with it. He often hung a brace of pheasants on the keeper's door to show his contempt. On one occasion he was seen by the head keeper of a certain noble Lord driving across a field with pheasant tail feathers sticking out of the back of his Land Rover. Apoplectic with rage the keeper rushed up, stopped him and demanded to see inside the vehicle. With a show of reluctance the poacher finally gave in and opened the door but the inside was empty, except for a row of cock pheasant tail feathers stuck into potatoes and lined up to stick out under the door!

The other is about an enterprising public school boy who used to take orders for game from the wives of housemasters. He poached it from local estates or the nearby river and his first-class service included delivering the game oven-ready. The problem of disposing of the feathers was soon overcome by going into the cellars and filling up the trunks of junior boys. Nemesis was waiting however, for at the end of term when the youngsters found their trunks full of feathers one of them had the bright idea of emptying them into a skip in the quadrangle. Unfortunately a wind got up during the night and blew the feathers everywhere. Surprisingly nothing was said, but I suppose the masters were reluctant for their source of game to dry up. I hasten to add that the young man is now a model husband and father and a very successful commodities broker.

Friends often ask me why when I cook pheasant it is not dry. My answer is to get a clay pot, be it a chicken brick or Romertoft. This rarely fails to produce succulent, juicy birds and can also be used with great success to cook venison, another meat which tends to dryness. Failing a clay pot, great attention to basting, braising or finding other moisture-enhancing ingredients is the answer.

Pheasant Terrine
with Mushrooms, Apple and Calvados

This delicious recipe was given to me when I was in Normandy visiting some stud farms on behalf of a bloodstock agency. I sometimes vary the recipe and substitute peeled, cooked chestnuts chopped in chunks, for the mushrooms.

Serves 4 - 6

---

1 uncooked pheasant
¼ pint (150ml) Calvados
1 thick slice white bread without the crusts
1 egg beaten with 3 tablespoons (45ml) milk
2 shallots, peeled and chopped
2 oz (50g) button mushrooms, sliced
1 oz (25g) butter
1 Cox's apple, peeled, cored and chopped
8 oz (250g) fat pork, minced
2 teaspoons fresh, chopped or 1 teaspoon dried
 tarragon
salt and freshly ground black pepper
6 rashers smoked, streaky bacon, de-rinded

Remove the breasts from the pheasants and cut them lengthways into thin slices. Lay them in a dish and marinate them in the Calvados for 2 hours. Cut the rest of the flesh off the bird and chop finely. Soak the bread in the egg and milk and sauté the shallots and mushrooms for a few seconds in the butter. Remove the slices of breast to a plate and mix the marinade with the soaked bread, shallots, mushrooms, apple, pork, herbs and seasoning. Flatten the rashers with the back of a knife, reserve two and line an oval or oblong 1½ pint (900ml) terrine with the rest. Fill the dish with alternate layers of mixture and breasts ending up with a final layer of mixture. Lay the remaining two rashers on top, cover with foil and place in a roasting pan. Pour in boiling water to come half way up the side of the terrine and place in a pre-heated oven set at 350F/Gas Mark 4/175C for 1½ hours.

Pierce with a skewer and press gently, if the liquid is clear, the terrine is cooked, if not put back for a further 15 minutes. When done, remove and place a weight on top until it is cold. Refrigerate for 2 days to let the flavours develop. Before serving decorate with a line of overlapping slices of sautéed mushroom and pour over a layer of aspic (see p163-4).

Pheasant soup with Onion and Chutney

You can make this soup quite easily from left-over roast pheasant carcasses. It is an excellent instance of 'progressive cookery'.

────────────── *Serves 4 – 6* ──────────────

1 large onion, peeled and chopped
1 oz (25g) butter
2 pints (1 litre) stock (see p.160) or stock cube
   and water
1 or 2 pheasant carcasses
1 tablespoon (15 ml) mango chutney
1 glass red wine
salt and pepper
1 pinch curry powder
beurre manié (see p.167)

Fry the onion slices in butter until brown and caramelized, add the stock and stir round. Transfer to a saucepan with all the other ingredients except the beurre manié. Cook until the liquid is reduced to 1½ pints (900ml). Strain through a colander, pick out all the bones and then liquidize. If too thin, bring to the boil and drop in small pieces of beurre manié (see p.167) whisking continuously until it is thick enough. If you want a consommé type of soup strain through a tea towel and if you don't mind the palaver, clarify it (see p.162).

Braised Pheasant with Lemon and Fennel

This recipe prevents the pheasant meat from drying out, and has the added advantage that you can cook it in the morning, or even the day before and heat it up just before serving.

——————— *Serves 4* ———————

4 oz (125g) butter
1 oven-ready pheasant
4 bulbs fennel
1 lemon
1 shallot
¼ pint (150ml) stock (see p.160) or stock cube
*   and water*
1 glass dry Martini
1 tablespoon (15 ml) fromage frais
salt and pepper

Melt the butter in a 3 pint (1.8 litre) cast iron, enamelled, casserole and brown the pheasant lightly. Remove it and add the trimmed fennel cut in thick horizontal slices and cook in the butter for a few minutes. Place the pheasant on top, squeeze over the lemon juice and put the shallot and squeezed half lemon inside the bird. Season well and pour in the stock and Martini. Cover tightly and cook in a pre-heated oven set at 350F/Gas Mark 4/180C for 1 – 1½ hours, or until tender, turning occasionally. When done, take out the pheasant, carve into slices and lay on top of the fennel which you have transferred to a serving dish. Degrease the remaining liquid, pour into a small pan and reduce by fast boiling to 2 fl oz (75ml). Remove from heat, stir in the fromage frais and spoon over the pheasant. Serve with rice.

If you have a chicken brick you can cook the pheasant (rubbed in oil) in this by placing the clay pot in a cold oven and turning the oven to 475F/Gas Mark 9/240C for 1 – 1½ hours. Cook the fennel in a saucepan with the butter, stock and Martini until tender and follow above serving instructions.

Nigerian Pheasant

This recipe was kindly given to me by the Editor of *The Field,* Jonathan Young. It was the main dish at a party he gave and was so popular that I think, if they could have got away with it, the guests would have licked the casserole clean. I have given the recipe as it was given to me with the ingredients and method in Jonathan's exact words.

'I was given this at a Roman Catholic mission in Gongola State, Nigeria. Our hosts, an Irish priest and nun, were spectacularly free with Star beer, the lethal local brew. Some of the ingredients were therefore lost in the resulting haze, and this is my home-grown version. It's designed to cope with Nigerian chicken, a long-legged beastie with the succulence of a dried out flannel. It is then, perfect for pheasants, especially, if like me you prefer skinning to plucking. The following recipe is for eight, since most of my friends travel in packs if they think there's a free meal. It re-heats brilliantly.

———————— *Serves 8* ————————

the meat from 4 pheasants
vegetable oil
¾ of a 1 lb (500g) jar of peanut butter
3 tablespoons (45ml) ground cumin
3 tablespoons (45ml) ground coriander
1 – 2 tablespoons (15 - 30ml) hot curry powder
3 teaspoons ground ginger
3 (420g) tins sliced peaches (in juice)
2 (432g) tins pineapple pieces (in juice)
3 chicken stock cubes
½ (200g) bar of creamed coconut
2 tablespoons (30ml) lime pickle (if handy)
salt and pepper
1 large handful salted peanuts
3 large bananas
1 lb (500g) long grain rice
2 tablespoons (30ml) ground turmeric (for rice)

Remove meat from the pheasants and cut into chunks. Put carcasses into a stock pot for soup. Put into a large pan the oil (about 3 gurgles' worth), peanut butter and spices. Heat until hot and add pheasant meat. Add more oil if necessary. After 5 minutes, add the tinned fruit, stock cubes and creamed coconut. Cook for a further 55 minutes, adjust seasoning, add the peanuts and sprinkle with chopped banana before serving.

Serve with rice boiled with turmeric (which gives it a splendid yellow colour and slightly dusty taste).'

Lucy's Pheasant and Lentil Stew

My daughter Lucy unearthed some pheasants at the bottom of her deep freeze which, she said, gave her a tired feeling so she decided to have a mass cook up before she was landed with the next batch. This is what she produced, and I have to say it is most succulent and is an excellent way of using up an old bird. If you are unable to get the brown lentils you can use 2 tins of green lentils. It is best made the day before and re-heated.

──────────── *Serves 4 – 6* ────────────

1 or 2 old pheasants
1 tablespoon (15ml) olive oil
1 pint (600ml) stock made from pheasant carcass
    (see p.160)
12 oz (350g) brown or green lentils, or 2 (432g)
    tins green lentils
1 onion peeled and stuck with 2 cloves
2 bay leaves
1 onion, carrot, stick celery peeled and chopped
2 cloves garlic peeled and chopped
4 oz (100g) fat bacon, diced
1 teaspoon herbes de Provence, or mixed herbs
2 glasses port
1 pkt (10g) dried porcini mushrooms soaked in
    hot stock (see p.160) to cover
salt and freshly ground black pepper

7

Remove meat from the pheasant(s), cut into chunks, marinate in the oil and make the stock (see p.160) from the carcass(es). Meanwhile bring the lentils to the boil with the onion stuck with cloves and the bay leaves and transfer to a casserole. Brown the pheasant chunks, bacon and chopped vegetables in some more oil and add them to the lentils. Pour in the stock, port and soaked porcini and season well. Place in a pre-heated oven at 400F/Gas Mark 6/200C for 20 minutes and then reduce heat to 300F/Gas Mark 3/160C for 2 – 3 hours or until the meat is tender. Look at it occasionally and if it seems dry add some water or stock.

Serve with Italian ciabatta bread and a green salad.

Pheasant Breasts au Gratin with Pasta

This is a quick and easy dish which takes care of the bird with mangled legs, or what, in the days when I was a game dealer my plucking ladies used to call 'dodgies'. You can either use the carcass(es) for soup or if really badly damaged, just skin and cut off the breasts.

———————— Serves 4 ————————

4 pheasant breasts
1 pint (600ml) stock (see p.160)
8 oz (250g) spaghetti or tagliatelle
1 oz (25g) butter
½ pint (300ml) double cream
4 oz (125g) grated Parmesan or pecorino
   cheese
1 pinch freshly grated nutmeg
salt and freshly ground black pepper.

Simmer the pheasant breasts very gently in the stock for 20 minutes. Cook the pasta, drain, toss in butter and transfer to a shallow fireproof dish and place the breasts in a single layer on top. Mix the cream, cheese and seasonings and spoon carefully over the breasts. Flash under a very hot grill so that the cream bubbles and browns a little and serve immediately. Spinach purée goes well with this.

Stir Fried Pheasant
with Shitake and Oyster Mushrooms

This is what I call an 'elastic quickie' which, translated, means 2 pheasant breasts stretched to feed 4 people. A wok is best, but if you haven't got one a frying pan will do.

—————————— *Serves 4* ——————————

2 raw pheasant breasts
sunflower oil
1 lb (500g) basmati rice
water
1 bunch spring onions, trimmed, cleaned and
   shredded
4 oz (125g) cauliflower florets
4 oz (125g) each shitake and oyster mushrooms,
   cut into strips (ordinary mushrooms can be used
   if you prefer)
Lea & Perrins ginger and orange sauce
soy sauce
salt and pepper
1 oz (25g) flaked almonds

Slice the pheasant breasts into thin strips. Heat a little oil in a saucepan, tip in the rice and shake well to coat the grains. Pour on boiling water to come 1" (2cm) above it, cover and cook over a very low heat until all the water is absorbed. Turn off the heat, cover with a tea towel folded in four and leave for 15 minutes. Heat about 1 tablespoon (15ml) of oil in wok or frying pan, toss in the onions and cauliflower and cook for a few minutes, shaking and stirring continuously, then add the pheasant strips and finally the mushrooms and cook for 2-3 minutes. Season with a good shake or two of the orange and ginger and soy sauce and salt and pepper. Mix in with the cooked rice, heat through, sprinkle over the almonds and serve.

Autumn Pudding

This is my version of summer pudding but made with all wild autumn fruits. If you do not have access to wild bilberries or whortleberries you can use a pack of bilberries from the supermarket.

——————————— *Serves 4 – 6* ———————————

½ lb (250g) peeled, cored crab apples or cooking apples cut in chunks
1½ lbs (750g) mixed blackberries, elderberries and bilberries
8 oz (250g) sugar
8 – 10 slices white bread, crusts removed

Cook the apples in 1 tablespoon (15ml) water tightly covered for a few minutes until just soft then add the rest of the fruit and sugar and cook over a very low heat until the juice runs. Line a 2 pint (1 litre) pudding basin with the bread and spoon in the fruit. Cover with more bread slices and pour over the rest of the juice. Stand in a dish to catch any juice that overflows, cover with a saucer or small plate and weight it down with a couple of (440g) tins of baked beans. Leave to cool and then refrigerate for 24 hours. Run a knife round the bowl and turn out.

Serve with Greek yoghurt.

Blackberry Whisky

This recipe was given to me by my plumber, a real countryman. I hate to think what happens when he is called out to repair a leaking pipe and sees an inviting blackberry bush. This liqueur has often fooled my in-house tasting panels and when asked to adjudicate between several brews, nine times out of ten it comes top of the list. Cooking blackberries seems to bring out the flavour while raw ones can be a bit disappointing, but marry them with whisky and sugar and you have a winner. So pack a plastic bag when you go out to get 'one for the pot' or browse along a leafy lane when you are out for a walk. You can, of course, use cultivated blackberries.

4 lbs (1.8kg) blackberries
8 oz (225g) cane sugar
1 bottle whisky

Place fruit, sugar and whisky in a large screw top jar. Shake every three or four days until the sugar has completely dissolved and then place in a dark cupboard for three months or until the whisky has turned a deep purple colour. Then strain and bottle. Keep its whereabouts secret for as long as a year, if possible.

PARTRIDGE

Twenty-five years ago Tom, a friend of ours, decided to leave city life and run a partridge shoot in Spain. The only man who had inside information as to which bits of ground might be available to rent was a well-known local poacher or *furtivo* called Fernando. His most successful method of poaching was to drive his battered old car along a road, spy a covey of partridges and stop and shoot one out of the window. His dog, Paloma would then be sent to retrieve it and would jump back into the by now moving car with her trophy. The whole operation being accomplished so quickly it was hopefully unseen by either landowner or policeman.

At that time in every bar you would see many stuffed birds, amongst which were different species of birds of prey, not then protected in Spain. The wife of one of Tom's party of guns was a keen ornithologist and was sent out with Fernando to a *laguna*, or lake, to see a rare variety of marsh harrier. Fernando dumped her and her companion at one end of the lake with their binoculars. Throughout the day they spotted no fewer than twenty-two of the birds, but to their astonishment every time one of them flew over there was a loud bang and the bird fell down. The mystery was soon explained, for when Tom's Land Rover returned to pick them up, to their horror they saw no fewer than eighteen corpses which Fernando was going to flog to the local taxidermist. Not their idea of a day's bird watching! This exploit took Tom a lot of living down.

There are two varieties of partridge, the English or grey partridge *Perdrix perdrix* and the French or redleg partridge *Alectoris rufa*. The wild English partridge plainly roasted on a piece of succulent and soggy toast is a gourmet's dream. The redleg partridge is also good but it is not in the same league and even when young tends to dryness, so great care must be taken when cooking it.

Sautéed Partridge Breasts with Madeira and Mushroom Sauce

This is a trouble-free idea for a dinner party as it saves the hostess the pain of seeing most of her beautifully cooked partridges left on the plate by guests who are unskilled at dissection. The legs can be frozen for use later.

—————————— *Serves 6* ——————————

butter for frying
6 partridge breasts coated in egg and breadcrumb
6 squares of bread fried in butter

Madeira and Mushroom Sauce

1 shallot, finely chopped
1 oz (25g) butter
2 oz (50g) mushrooms, thinly sliced
½ pint (300ml) game or chicken stock (see p.160)
1 glass Madeira
a few drops of sherry vinegar
salt and pepper
beurre manié (see p.167)

Heat the butter until foaming and shallow fry the partridge breasts until golden brown on each side. Place on a heated serving dish on the squares of fried bread. For the sauce, cook the shallots in butter until transparent and then add the mushrooms and cook for a few seconds then remove onto a plate. Pour in the stock and Madeira and reduce by fast boiling to ¼ pint (150ml), tip back the mushrooms and shallots, season and whisk in a few bits of beurre manié (see p.167) to thicken very slightly. Taste and add one or two drops of sherry vinegar.

Serve with new potatoes and carrot and watercress purée.

Paella del Campo

In the early days of Tom's Spanish shooting venture everything was pretty basic. Locomotion between drives was either on foot or muleback. The magnificent grey horses were ridden by the keepers and not by lesser mortals such as us. Everyone had a nickname as the Spaniards could not pronounce our names. '*El remolacho*' (the beetroot) had a red face, '*el gordo*' (the greedy one) was large and fat, '*el guapo*' (the beautiful one) was rather plain and so on. Lunch came down in panniers by mule and, apart from the rice, salt and pepper, sweet peppers, oil, bread and wine everything else was produced from the *campo* or countryside. The partridges would have been shot by the party, a rabbit perhaps caught by the beaters and the herbs plucked from the rocky hillside. The mingled smells of rosemary, thyme, lavender and cistus were quite overwhelming. As the venue was probably by a stream running through a deep gorge with mountains stretching away in the distance while up in the sky a rare raptor was soaring in the thermals, it was quite unforgettable.

This is my version.

———— Serves 6 - 8 ————

olive oil
2 garlic cloves, peeled and chopped
1 onion, peeled and chopped
1 sweet red pepper de-seeded and cut into strips
2 oven-ready French partridges, jointed and cut
   up
a dash of brandy (Spanish Fundador, if posssible)
1 lb (500g) pullao rice (the nearest you will get to
   Spanish rice)
water
1 chicken stock cube
2 sprigs each fresh rosemary, thyme and marjoram,
   (or 1 teaspoon each dried)
salt and pepper

Heat the oil in the paella pan, large frying pan or wok until it is smoking then throw in the garlic, onion, peppers and partridge joints to brown. You can add anything else you like; sometimes a rabbit would go in and some wild mushrooms and, on one never to be forgotten occasion, a couple of magpies, but I don't advocate this. When everything has browned slosh in some brandy, then the rice, stir it all round and add the water, crumbled stock cube, herbs, salt, pepper and as much saffron as you can afford. Let it bubble steadily, give it the odd stir and add more water if it looks like drying out too much.

When the rice is cooked serve with plenty of *pain de campagne* (French country bread, obtainable in some supermarkets) and lots of Spanish red wine; the *Marqués de Cacerés* goes particularly well. I've never tried it but I am sure you could cook this dish on a barbecue. To be authentic you could hand round *prosciutto* with the bread. In Spain we had *taco*, the same sort of thing only cut in thick chunks and your teeth had to be in pretty good shape to chew it. We used to see it hanging up drying in the air outside. Not for nothing did we christen it biltong!

Katie's Partridge with Olives and Bacon

Twenty-five years on and things in Spain are much more civilized. Tom has built a house where he and his wife Katie live. She is no mean cook and this is what she gives the guests.

———————— Serves 4 ————————

6 oz (150g) butter
4 oven-ready young French partridges
2 rashers bacon, finely chopped
4 fl oz (100ml) red wine
1½ pint (300ml) brown sauce
8 oz (250g) pitted black olives, cut into 4
salt and pepper

Brown Sauce

butter for frying
1 carrot, 1 onion, 1 leek, peeled and
*   chopped into dice*
1 pint (600ml) game stock (see p.160)
1 bouquet garni consisting of a sprig of parsley,
*   thyme and marjoram*
salt and pepper

Make the sauce ahead of time; you can freeze it. Heat some butter and fry the vegetables until they are brown, add the stock and simmer gently for ¾ - 1 hour, then strain, pressing well to extract all the juice from the vegetables. Skim off fat with squares of kitchen paper and reduce to ½ pint (300ml). Pre-heat the oven to 400F/Gas Mark 6/200C. Melt the butter until foaming and coat the birds well in it. Roast them for 20 - 30 minutes until they are tender, don't overcook. When pierced with a skewer the juice should be clear. Cut in half and dish up onto a serving dish and keep warm. Fry the bacon in the pan juices, add the red wine and brown sauce and reduce to ¼ pint (150ml). Add the olives, adjust seasoning and pour over the partridges.

Serve with sauté potatoes and red cabbage.

Leicester Casserole

Here is the English answer to the Spanish peasant dish of Paella del Campo. No doubt in times past the partridges would have been netted by a poacher who, perhaps passing a field of cabbages on the way home, would have nicked one. Anyway, in modern times it is an excellent method of cooking old birds of either species.

———————— *Serves 6* ————————

3 large onions, cut in chunks
2 large carrots, peeled and cut in rounds
1 small tin (220g) butter beans
8 oz (250g) fat bacon, cut into cubes
3 shallots, peeled
3 rashers streaky bacon
3 oven-ready old partridges
1 whole cabbage, blanched and cut in 4
1 pint (600ml) boiling milk
stock (see p.160) or 1 chicken stock cube dissolved
  in ¼ pint (150ml) water
2 teaspoons each fresh parsley and thyme, chopped,
  or 1 teaspoon dried
salt and pepper

Tip the onions, carrots, beans and bacon into a casserole. Put a shallot inside each bird and lay a bacon rasher over the breast. Sit them on the bed of vegetables. Stuff the cabbage quarters round the outside and pour over the boiling milk and stock, season with herbs, salt and pepper and cook in a pre-heated oven at 325F/Gas Mark 3/160C for 2 – 3 hours or until tender.

Serve with plain boiled potatoes.

Partridges Braised with Quince and Honey

If you don't have a readily available source of quinces use apple instead. True quince *Cydonia oblonga* is best with its fragrant golden pear-shaped fruits and it is really worth planting for both its beauty and culinary excellence. The other kind is *Chaenomeles japonica* which with its attractive coral or red flowers is often seen growing up the front of cottage or house; its fruits are also edible though not quite so strong.

─────────── *Serves 4 - 6* ───────────

2 oz (50g) butter
3 young oven-ready partridges
3 rashers bacon, de-rinded and chopped
4 shallots, peeled and finely chopped
6 oz (175g) quince, peeled and cut up
½ pint (300ml) stock (see p.160) or stock cube and water
1 glass white wine
salt and pepper
honey
2 tablespoons crème fraîche

Heat the butter in a casserole and put in the birds, bacon, shallots and quince. Cook for a few seconds, stirring and shaking, then pour in the stock and wine and season with salt and pepper. Put in a pre-heated oven set at 350F/Gas Mark 4/180C for 1½ hours or until tender. (If the birds are old, cook at 325F/Gas Mark 3/160C for 2 – 3 hours.) Cut up and arrange on a dish. Reduce the sauce, add honey to taste, liquidize and return to pan. Re-heat and stir in the crème fraîche then spoon over the partridges.
Serve with croquette potatoes and tiny french beans.

Chaudfroid of Partridge Breasts Elizabeth

I was stuck for a good summer dish so I adapted this one, which is normally served hot. It really is delicious and could easily be used for pheasant breasts, although I would probably slice them in half lengthways to make them thinner.

———————— *Serves 2 - 4* ————————

2 oz (50g) butter
4 partridge breasts, skinned
1 tablespoon (15ml) brandy
¼ pint (150ml) stock (see p.160)
salt and pepper
8 oz (250g) white grapes, peeled and de-seeded
½ pint (300ml) cream
*4 teaspoons aspic granules dissolved in a little
    boiling water (see p.)*
whole grapes to decorate

Melt the butter and sauté the breasts then pour in the warmed brandy and set alight. When the flames have died down add the stock, salt and pepper, cover and cook very gently for 20 minutes then add the skinned grapes and cream and cook for a further 5 minutes. Remove breasts to a plate, cover with clingfilm, leave to cool and then refrigerate. Add the aspic to the sauce and let it get cold. When it is just beginning to set spoon it over the breasts.

To serve, arrange on a dish and decorate with whole grapes. Accompany with a salad of dandelion, rocket and lettuce, and Pink Fir Apple, Belle de Fontenay or any other salad potato boiled and then tossed in walnut oil and lemon juice.

Strawberry Charlotte

This decorative sweet could also be made with raspberries or loganberries.

———————— *Serves 4 - 6* ————————

1 lb (500g) strawberries, hulled and washed
juice of half a lemon
4 oz (125g) sugar
½ pint (300ml) crème fraîche
20 boudoir biscuits, approximately
1 tablespoon (15ml) liqueur
¼ pint (150ml) water

Sprinkle the strawberries with 3 oz (75g) of the sugar and the lemon juice. Beat the crème fraîche until firm and add the remaining sugar, a little at a time. Incorporate the strawberries. Moisten the biscuits lightly in the liqueur and water, and line a 1 pint (600ml) soufflé dish with them. Spoon in the strawberry mixture and cover the top with some more moistened biscuits. Refrigerate overnight.

Turn it out on to a serving dish and surround with hulled strawberries.

GROUSE

Long ago, in the days of reapers and binders, some of the crofters in Sutherland used to concentrate on the 'grouse harvest'. The oat or barley stooks near the moor would be left standing bedraggled in the rain long after most farmers had their harvest safely in. "Look at those lazy Highlanders," it would be said, "they can't even be bothered to bring in the end of the harvest." But hidden in the stooks would be snares, and the crofters could enjoy a long season of grouse taken on their own land. Wouldn't you prefer grouse to an extra bowl of porridge?

If asked what was my favourite game-bird gastronomically, I would find it difficult to choose between a succulent young roast grouse or English partridge but I think on balance I would choose the grouse as here is a truly wild bird, denizen of the heather-clad hills. For some of us sitting in the comfort of our homes eating a tender young grouse memories will flood in of wonderful days in the highlands when you truly believe that nothing could ever be as beautiful as the panoramas which constantly unfold as you move from one line of butts to the next. There will be other memories too of wet, windy days when you sit shivering while the rain pours down and you are standing up to your ankles in water and peat, and yet again when you have walked all day with a few friends and their dogs, falling into peat hags and scrambling over rocks for only two or three brace. The wonderful flavour of these birds comes from the diet of heather buds, bilberries and wild cranberries on which they live.

If you are the recipient of a brace of grouse the chances are that they will be young but to make sure you can check, as follows. Hold the bird up by its beak; if it buckles under the weight and if the skull gives when you press it then you have a young bird. Old birds have unyielding beaks and skulls and very pronounced white, feathery 'spats'.

Basic Grouse Soup

This soup is very adaptable as you start off with a consommé which can either be eaten hot or, with the addition of gelatine, can become consommé en gelée. If a thick soup is the order of the day the addition of beurre manié and the other ingredients I have suggested below, will transform it into something quite different.

———— *Serves 6 - 8* ————

1 tablespoon (15ml) sunflower oil
4 carcasses of grouse, cooked or raw
2 oz (50g) diced, fat bacon
1 carrot, onion, leek, and celery stalk peeled
and chopped
1½ pints (900ml) game stock (see p.160), or
chicken stock cube and water
½ pint (300ml) red wine
1 glass sherry
1 teaspoon redcurrant jelly
1 tablespoon (15ml) sunflower oil
6 crushed juniper berries
½ teaspoon dried thyme
salt and pepper

Pre-heat oven and set at 450F/Gas Mark 8/230C. Pour the oil into a roasting pan and when it is hot add the grouse carcasses, bacon and vegetables. Shake to coat with the oil and allow to brown. Remove from the oven and transfer to a saucepan. Swill the pan out with the stock, wine and sherry and add to the grouse and vegetables with the other ingredients. Bring to the boil and simmer for 2 – 3 hours, skimming off any scum period-ically. Strain into a bowl and blot off any fat with kitchen paper. Adjust seasoning and serve as it is, or clarify it (see p.162).

Grouse Consommé En Gelée

To the above add 0.04oz (11g) gelatine dissolved in the sherry (see p.163). When set, spoon into soup cups and garnish with a blob of cream cheese topped by a speck of bilberry conserve.

Thick, Rich Grouse Soup

Heat the basic brew and whisk in small pieces of beurre manié (see p.167) until the right consistency is obtained. Then mix in 1 tablespoon (15ml) concentrated tomato purée and a dash of mushroom ketchup. As a variation you can add a few sautéed. sliced mushrooms, or some diced, cooked carrot or swede. Hand round croûtons of bread fried in bacon fat.

23

Traditional Roast Grouse

This has to be my favourite way of cooking grouse and I make no apology for including it as people so often ask me how I do it. You will wonder why I make 2 grouse serve 4 people. The answer is that nowadays people do not seem to have such huge appetites so I usually serve half a bird each.

At the risk of being accused of sexism I have met few men who are good at dissecting birds or fish. In fact it used to be a standing joke that wherever we dined, if my late husband Archie was served with a whole bird he would hand me his plate to deal with. For ease of carving I always remove the wishbone from any uncooked bird.

—————————— *Serves 2 - 4* ——————————

1 tablespoon (15ml) cranberries
4 rashers streaky bacon, de-rinded
2 oven-ready young grouse
4 oz (125g) butter
4 thick slices white bread, toasted, crusts cut off
1 tablespoon (15ml) warmed whisky
1 teaspoon cranberry jelly
¼ pint (150ml) game stock (see p.160) or
*   chicken stock cube and water*
salt and pepper

Pre-heat the oven and set at 400F/Gas Mark6/200C. Place half the cranberries in each grouse and cover with the rashers. Melt the butter in the roasting pan until it is foaming, put in the birds and baste well. Roast for 1 hour, basting every 15 – 20 minutes, then remove the bacon. Sit the birds on the toast and roast for a further 10 minutes until the breasts are browned. Slice off each breast together with the leg and thigh and place on half a piece of toast. Arrange on a serving dish. Pour the warmed whisky into the roasting pan and set it alight; then stir in the stock, add the jelly, adjust the seasoning and pour into a gravy boat.

Serve with 4 to 6 oatcakes crushed and fried until golden in bacon fat or butter, bread sauce, game chips and diced cooked turnips tossed in butter and brown sugar until the sugar caramelizes and turns toffee-like.

Pan Fried Young Grouse Breast with Sauce Bercy

Grouse being a rich, dark meat goes particularly well with Sauce Bercy which is usually served with fried steak. The sharpness of the lemon juice 'cuts across the fat' as my mother's old cook used to put it so succinctly.

———————— *Serves 4* ————————

4 raw, young grouse breasts, skinned
flour for dredging
butter for frying
4 croûtons fried bread
salt and pepper

Sauce Bercy

2 oz (50g) shallots, finely chopped
½ pint (300ml) dry white wine
grouse livers, lightly sautéed
3 tablespoons butter
2 tablespoons (30ml) finely chopped parsley
juice of ½ a lemon

Dust the breasts lightly with flour and sauté in foaming butter for 3 minutes on each side. Place them on the croûtons, season lightly with salt and pepper and keep warm on a serving dish. For the sauce, simmer the shallots and white wine until reduced to about ⅛ of a pint (75ml). Place in the food processor with the livers, parsley, lemon juice and butter. Spoon over the grouse and serve with new potatoes and a green salad to which you have added a few leaves of sorrel. You can replace the white wine by red wine but it then becomes *Sauce Marchand de Vin*. It is equally good with sautéed pigeon breasts or slices of roe fillet.

Rich Grouse Pie

This is perfect for using old grouse, which are much cheaper. Maturity makes for a rich strong flavour and the recipe is a perfect example of what I call 'progressive cookery'. The first stage can be eaten in its own right and the remainder made into the pie. If you do this you may have to increase the number of grouse or else make a smaller pie. As the size of grouse varies I cannot be precise about the quantity of grouse meat so you will have to weigh it and then divide by two to get the weight of butter. A rough guide would be 8oz (225g) meat per bird.

———— Serves 4 - 6 ————

the meat from 4 uncooked old grouse, skinned and cut into 1" (5cm) cubes. (This will produce approximately 1½ lbs (750g) meat)
salt, pepper
1 pinch each of ground ginger, cinnamon and nutmeg
4 fl oz (150ml) port or red wine
½ the weight of the grouse meat in butter
1 lb (500g) pork sausage meat
½ pint (300ml) concentrated stock (see p.160)
1 teaspoon redcurrant jelly
0.04 oz (11g) gelatine or ½ oz (15g) aspic (see p.163)
forcemeat balls (see p.159)
shortcrust pastry using 6 oz (175g) flour (see p.164)
1 egg, well beaten

Season the grouse meat liberally with the salt, pepper and spices and put into a straight-sided casserole or earthenware or china jar with the port and butter. Cover tightly with foil and a lid and stand in a saucepan of boiling water, to reach half way up the side of the casserole or jar, and cook on top of the stove for 3 hours or until tender. Allow to get quite cold and skim off the layer of butter which will have formed on top. (You can use this for grouse pâté). Mix the forcemeat ingredients (see p.159), shape into 12 balls and fry lightly. Spread the sausagemeat on the base of a 2 pint (1 litre) pie dish, stand a pie funnel in the middle and surround with the cooled grouse meat. Dot with the forcemeat balls. Pour on the cooking juices and cover and decorate with the pastry, then brush with the beaten egg. Make a hole in the top and bake in a pre-heated oven set at 400F/Gas Mark 6/200C for 35 minutes. Dissolve the jelly and gelatine (or aspic) (see p.163) in the stock then pour it through the hole in the pastry.

Serve hot with a purée of celeriac and new potatoes, or cold with watercress salad.

Bread Sauce

In our family bread sauce is mandatory with grouse, partridge or pheasant but so often expectations are dashed when you are given a roast bird, be it in a friend's house or in a restaurant and it is not forthcoming. Not long ago I received a telephone call from a young friend saying he had some pheasants roasting in the oven and asking for my bread sauce recipe, so here it is.

―――――――――― *Serves 4 - 6* ――――――――――

1 pint (600ml) milk
1 onion, peeled and cut in chunks
2 cloves (optional)
6 slices white bread, crusts cut off
1 oz (25g) butter
salt and plenty of freshly ground black pepper

Bring the milk, onion and cloves to the boil. Whizz the bread in the food processor or crumble roughly and add the fresh breadcrumbs to the milk. Stir, season with salt and pepper cover with buttered paper or foil and then a lid. Leave to sit on the edge of the stove until required. Just before using beat in the butter (my daughter Lucy also adds a dollop of cream). You can make the sauce in the morning and reheat it. For those who don't fancy chunks of onion, simply stick the cloves into the whole onion, let it sit in the sauce and remove it just before serving. If you don't like the taste of cloves, try infusing a bay leaf in the milk instead.

Cranberry Sauce

Wild cranberries are fantastic but you can rarely pick enough on a moor so you will probably have to make do with the cultivated ones which are widely available in big supermarkets.

——————— Serves 4 – 6 ———————
8 oz (250g) cranberries
water to cover
runny honey to taste

Place the cranberries in a pan, barely cover with water and simmer until they have burst and are mushy. Stir in honey to taste and cook for a few minutes longer. Cool. Any left-over sauce should be frozen as it will not keep.

Bilberry Chranachan

This is particularly delicious with wild bilberries, cranberries, or wild rasberries and as you don't have to use many it may even be possible to pick them yourself; otherwise replace with any slightly tart berry. Wild rasberries are found not only in Scotland but may also be seen growing in the south of England at the edge of woods; you just have to know where to look.

—————————— *Serves 4 - 6* ——————————

6 coarse oatcakes
1 tablespoon (15ml) whisky or Drambuie
½ pint (300ml) cream, stiffly whipped
¼ pint (105ml) Greek yoghurt,
4 oz (125g), or thereabouts, berries of your
  choice
1 tablespoon (15ml) sugar

Crush the oatcakes and crisp them in a hot oven set at 400F/Gas Mark 6/200C for about 10 minutes, but keep a beady eye on them as they burn easily. Add the whisky to the whipped cream and then the yoghurt and sugar, but watch out that it does not become sloppy. Lastly, fold in the oatcakes and berries. Serve immediately.

WILD DUCK

There is nothing more magical than waiting in the pre-dawn or the gloaming by a river, loch or on the fore-shore for a morning or evening duck flight to come in. The sense of achievement when your prize is steaming on the table is all the greater, as the shots taken seem almost impossible. Wild duck is a blanket description, and there are many species, but the ones most commonly encountered are mallard, teal and wigeon and the first is the only variety you are likely to see on the supermarket shelf.

Roast Mallard with Honey and Quince

There is little fat beneath the skin of a wild duck so, if you are roasting them, a covering of honey will help you to get a crisp outside. If you don't have a quince tree use crab apples or tart cooking apples.

──────── Serves 4 ────────

2 mallard
2 shallots, peeled and chopped
2 quinces, peeled, cored and chopped
4 oz (125g) butter
salt and pepper
2 tablespoons runny honey
salt and pepper
¼ pint (150ml) cider

Leave the ducks in a cold airy place for 24 hours or, uncovered, in the fridge. Sauté the shallots and quince in a little of the butter until soft and spoon into the body cavities. Prick all over and rub with salt, then cover with honey. Pre-heat the oven to 400F/Gas Mark 6/200C and heat the remaining butter in a roasting pan until foaming. Put in the duck and baste well. Baste again after 15 minutes then pour on some more honey and roast for a further 30 – 45 minutes until tender and crisp. When cooked, remove to a serving dish, having first scraped out the stuffing. Swill out the roasting pan with cider, add to the quince and whizz in the food processor. Pour into a sauce boat.

Serve with allumette potatoes and steamed cauliflower florets.

Easy Casserole of Wild Duck with Orange

If you want a no-hassle recipe this is really easy and is much more delicious when re-heated the next day. Unfortunately one of the original ingredients, Baxter's Duck and Orange Soup is no longer made, but their Game Soup makes a good substitute. I don't have an Aga but for those who have this is wonderful cooked in the bottom oven.

──────────── Serves 4 - 6 ────────────

2 oranges
2 mallard
2 (425g) tins Baxter's Game Soup
12 pickling onions, peeled and kept whole
     (small onions or shallots will do as a sub-
     stitute)
2 glasses red wine
salt and pepper
2 teaspoons potato or cornflour mixed with a
     little water

Halve the oranges and stick a half inside each duck. Place the birds in a casserole with all the other ingredients plus the juice from the remaining orange halves and season well. Place in a pre-heated oven set at 400F/Gas Mark 6/200C for 15 minutes then turn down to 325F/Gas Mark 3/160C for a further 45 minutes or until tender. Remove and leave to get cold. Skim off fat, cut meat off ducks. Thicken the sauce with the potato or cornflour, season to taste and re-heat the duck gently in it.

Serve with brown rice and chicory salad.

Mike Swan's Chinese Gingered Duck

This delicious concoction was given to me by Mike Swan of the Game Conservancy. He is no mean cook and I am indebted to him for several unusual recipes. This is ideal for those who quail at the thought of plucking a duck. All you have to do is to skin the breasts and cut them off.

―――――――――――― *Serves 4 - 6* ――――――――――

4 duck breasts, sliced thinly
2 oz (50g) fresh ginger root, peeled and cut
  into fine strips
2 tablespoons (30ml) oil
2 oz (50g) flaked almonds
2 cloves garlic, crushed
2 tablespoons (30ml) soy sauce
2 tablespoons (30ml) dry sherry
4 spring onions, finely shredded

Mix the duck with the ginger and leave covered for half an hour. Heat the oil in a wok or frying pan and cook the almonds until golden brown. Transfer them to a plate with a slotted spoon. Add garlic to the pan and then the duck and ginger and stir fry for about 5 minutes or until the duck is just cooked. Add all the other ingredients except the almonds and cook over a high heat for a few seconds. Sprinkle the almonds on top and serve with egg noodles, beansprouts and fine green beans.

Mallard with Caramel Sauce

This is a delicious way of cooking wild duck and is a really successful example of marrying the sweet with the sour.

——————— Serves 6 ———————

salt and pepper
2 wild duck
2 sprigs of rosemary
4 oz (125g) butter
1 lb (500g) new potatoes
1 lb (500g) small turnip, peeled and left whole
4 tablespoons (60ml) olive oil
4 tablespoons (60ml) demerara sugar
4 tablespoons (60ml) red wine vinegar
1 tablespoon (15 ml) strong French mustard
water

Salt and pepper the two duck and put a rosemary sprig inside each. Baste with melted butter and roast in a pre-heated oven set at 400F/Gas Mark 6/200C for 30 – 45 minutes. Meanwhile cook the potatoes and turnips until just tender, drain and sauté separately in a mixture of butter and oil until golden brown. When the turnips start to colour sprinkle with a little sugar and cook until caramelized. When the birds are cooked remove to a serving dish. Dissolve the sugar in a small saucepan with a little water and boil, without stirring, to make a dark caramel. Take off the heat and carefully add 1 tablespoon of water. Degrease the roasting tin, add the caramel, vinegar, mustard, salt and pepper and stir well, it should taste hot and sweet. Pour over the ducks and surround with the potatoes and turnips.

Sheila's Damson Duck

When I launched my first cookery book at the Floors Game Fair in Scotland, a lady came up to me and said, "I hate cooking, so I shan't be buying your book, but I have got a rather good way of doing duck and you are welcome to the recipe. It all came about because my husband and I had just bottled our damson gin and felt it was a waste to throw away the fruit, so I just used them for stuffing the wild duck which my husband had shot." I have made a few alterations, but it really is quite delicious. If you haven't made any damson gin, try sloes. Pigeon are also good done this way.

————————— Serves 4 - 6 —————————

salt and pepper
2 mallard
4 tablespoons (60ml) gin or vodka-sodden
    damsons or sloes
2 shallots, peeled
4 oz (125g) butter
¼ pint (150ml) stock (see p.160) or chicken
    stock cube and water
½ teaspoon cornflour or potato flour
a few drops of balsamic, sherry or red wine
    vinegar

Salt and pepper the duck inside and out and stuff with your chosen alcoholic fruit and the shallots. Set the oven at 425F/Gas Mark 7/220C and melt the butter in a roasting tin. Put the ducks in and roast for 45 minutes to 1 hour, basting frequently. Carve onto a warmed serving dish. De-grease the roasting pan, add the stock and vinegar and let it bubble. Press as much of the fruit through a strainer as possible and add the purée. Thicken with the cornflour if necessary and pour over the carved duck.

A purée of potato into which you have incorporated diced cooked celeriac and chopped parsley makes a nice contrast in colour and taste.

Tyrolean Teal

Teal are very attractive, small duck which have more than a culinary appeal. The charming collective noun for a party of teal is a 'spring'. When you are waiting for them in some reed bed at dusk you hear the beat of their wings and almost before you know it they have spiralled down onto the water and unless you are very alert you will have missed your shot.

Quite why this should be called Tyrolean Teal is a mystery. The recipe was given to me by an old friend whose cook had served it up before the war and she had no idea where it came from. Whatever its provenance it is very good. As the birds are very small you will need half per person.

———————————— *Serves 4* ————————————

2 teal
2 - 4 (30 - 60ml) tablespoons stewed apple
  infused with cinnamon and mace
1 oz (25g) butter
4 tablespoons (60ml) red wine vinegar
1 good pinch sugar
salt and pepper
4 croûtons of fried bread

Pre-heat the oven to 400F/Gas Mark 6/200C. Stuff the teal with the apple mixture and place in a roasting pan. Bring the butter, vinegar, sugar, pepper and salt to the boil and baste the birds with it. Put in the oven and roast for 30 minutes, or until tender, basting frequently. Serve on croûtons of fried bread and pour over the sauce.

Serve with sauté potatoes and sugar snap peas.

Braised Teal with Gooseberry Sauce

Gooseberries are often used in France as an accompaniment to game and they go particularly well with teal.

———————— *Serves 4* ————————

2 teal
salt and pepper
2 oz (50g) butter
1 glass white wine
8 oz (250g) gooseberries
sugar to taste

Season the teal with salt and pepper and brown in a little butter in a fireproof casserole. Cover and place in a pre-heated oven set at 350F/Gas Mark 4/175C for 1 hour or until tender. Transfer to a heated serving dish. Cook the gooseberries in the wine until mushy. Blot the fat off the pan juices and add the gooseberries to it. Heat through and sweeten to taste then whizz in the food processor and pour into a sauceboat.

Serve with small potatoes steamed in their skins and cooked celery tossed in butter.

Teal with Lemon

In summer this recipe can be adapted for the barbecue. Use birds from your deep freeze as they are not in season until September.

————————— *Serves 6* —————————

*8 oz (250g) chicken livers (including livers from
   the teal)*
8 oz (250g) butter
*½ teaspoon Quatre Épices (a blend of pepper, nut-
   meg, cloves and cinnamon)*
salt and pepper
3 lemons
3 teal
6 rashers streaky bacon, de-rinded
6 - 8 thick slices bread, toasted

Sauté the livers in a little butter until cooked but still pink. Chop finely, season with Quatre Épices, (either bought or home ground), salt and pepper and the grated rind of two of the lemons. Stuff the birds with this mixture. Place a piece of lemon peel over each breast and wrap each teal in 2 bacon rashers. Enclose the birds in foil and make into 3 parcels. Roast in a pre-heated oven set at 425F/Gas Mark 7/220C for 30 - 40 minutes. Butter the toast whilst still hot. Remove the birds carefully from the foil, saving the juice, and cut in half. Scrape the stuffing onto the toast and place the teal halves on top. Pour over the juice and serve with new potatoes and a salad of frisée dressed with walnut oil and lemon juice and sprinkled with a few chopped, skinned walnuts.

Lady Durham's Sauce for Wild Duck

This recipe is dated 1904. One of the ingredients is Harveys Sauce, which is no longer available, but it still tastes pretty good and contrasts well with the richness of the duck.

pan juices from a roast duck
1 lemon, squeezed
4 tablespoons (60ml) Lea & Perrins
*   Worcestershire Sauce*
3 tablespoons (45ml) port wine
1 good dash of cayenne pepper
salt
1 - 2 tablespoons (15 - 30ml) stock (see p.160),
*   or water and a stock cube*

Add all the ingredients to the pan juices and bubble for a few seconds, scraping in the brown bits. Add stock, then pour into a sauceboat.

Mrs Watkins' Runner Bean Chutney

Before the days of freezers innumerable ways were employed to use up gluts of vegetable or fruit. This recipe was given to me by the farmer's wife, Mrs Watkins, who lives on the estate belonging to Archie's cousin, where we spent many happy hours 'flighting duck'. It was so good when I tasted it that I was unwilling to believe that the principle ingredient was runner bean.

Makes 4 - 6 x 1lb (500g) pots.

*2 lbs (1 kg) runner beans, de-stringed and
   sliced
1 lb (500g) onions, peeled and chopped
1 lb (500g) demerara sugar
1 pint (600ml) spiced vinegar
1 tablespoon (15ml) cornflour
1 tablespoon (15ml) mustard powder
1 tablespoon (15ml) turmeric*

Spiced Vinegar

*2 pints (1.2 litres) malt vinegar
1 oz (25g) mixed pickling spice*

First make the spiced vinegar. Put the vinegar and spices in a saucepan, cover and bring slowly to the boil. Remove from the heat and leave to cool, then strain and pour into clean, sterilized bottles. For the chutney: Cook the sliced beans until tender and then drain. Combine with the onions, sugar and all but 2 table-spoons (30ml) of the spiced vinegar in a saucepan and cook for 15 minutes. Mix dry ingredients to a smooth paste with the remaining vinegar, add to saucepan and boil until thick. Pour into heated screw-top jars, cover with clingfilm, and when cold put on screw tops.

Apple and Marrow Pie

This takes care of any glut of apples and marrows or even pumpkin and is a good pudding to serve at the beginning of the duck shooting season, perhaps after a dish of teal.

———————— *Serves 4 - 6* ————————

1 lemon
1 lb (500g) peeled, de-seeded and diced
   marrow or pumpkin
1 lb (500g) apples, peeled, cored and sliced
2 oz (50g) seedless raisins
1 stick cinnamon
2 tablespoons honey (thick or thin)
1 lemon
shortcrust pastry made with 6 oz (175g)
   plain flour (see p.164)
1 egg, beaten

Grate the lemon and mix together the marrow/pumpkin, apple and raisins and spoon into a pie dish, heaping it in the middle. Bury the cinnamon stick in the fruit. Stir the honey into the lemon juice and pour over. Make the pastry. Cover the pie, decorate with pastry leaves and make a couple of slits. Brush with the egg and sprinkle on some sugar. Preheat oven to 400F/Gas Mark 6/200C and cook for 1 hour.

WILD GOOSE

Archie was not very keen on shooting geese and the only time I went with him was in Austria in the early sixties. The shoot to which he was invited was on a lake through the centre of which ran the border with Hungary and we could see the watch towers of the Iron Curtain on the far side. The outing was tinged with sadness as although we saw quantities of geese, and Archie shot a couple, there were several bursts of automatic gunfire from the border guards and we wondered, but never knew, if some poor wretch had been trying to escape.

If your loved one comes home bearing a goose, my advice is to insist that he plucks it as you need fingers and thumb of cast iron and it is not a job for beautifully manicured nails. You must hope that he has not shot the leader of the skein as it will probably be as old as Methuselah. To get rid of the fishy taste you should straight away cut off the parson's nose and preening gland which is situated just behind it. Wash out the body cavity and insert an onion stuck with cloves and a crust of bread and leave for several hours, then remove before launching into your favourite recipe. The other treatment is to plunge the plucked goose into a preserving pan of boiling water to which you have added 1 tablespoon (15ml) of salt and 1 teaspoon of bicarbonate of soda. Leave for 2 minutes and then remove and dry well. Geese vary in weight according to species and age so you may be landed with anything from 6 - 10 lbs (2.5 - 5 kg).

Victoria's Way with Goose

Victoria's husband is a dedicated wildfowler and after many years of trial and error this is what she considers her best recipe.

──────────── *Serves 6 - 8* ────────────

1 goose, (plucked and drawn)
salt and ground black pepper
1 lb (500g) chopped, stoned prunes
1 lb (500g) cooking apples, peeled, cored and
  chopped
2 oz (50g) soft brown sugar
4 oz (100g) butter
1 large onion cut in thick rings
2 tablespoons (30 ml) redcurrant jelly
½ pint (300ml) stock made from the giblets
  (excluding the liver)
1 pint (600ml) dry cider

Rub the inside of the goose with salt and pepper. Mix together the prunes, apples and sugar and spoon into the body cavity. Roasting times depend on the size of the goose but a good guide is 20 minutes per lb (500g) plus 20 minutes for a bird weighing 5 lbs (2½kg) and 25 minutes per lb (500g) over this weight. Pre-heat the oven to 375F/Gas Mark 5/190C and melt the butter in a roasting tin until foaming. Put in the onion rings and place the goose on top. Spread with 1 tablespoon (15ml) of the jelly, season with salt and pepper and baste with the butter. Place on the centre runner of the oven and roast for 30 minutes. Bring stock and cider to the boil and add to the roasting tin. Reduce heat to 300F/Gas Mark2/150C and baste every 20 minutes. At the end of the cooking time pierce the leg with a skewer; if the juice runs clear it is done. Transfer bird to a warmed serving dish, add the other tablespoon of jelly to the roasting pan and reduce until the sauce looks thick and syrupy.

Serve with plain boiled or mashed potatoes and courgettes.

Francatelli's Goose with Horseradish Sauce

This recipe comes from a cookery book published in the 1800s by Francatelli who was a pupil of Carême and head chef to Queen Victoria. No fear of a fishy taste here, the marinade takes care of that and the horseradish sauce puts the finishing touch.

———————— *Serves 6 - 8* ————————

1 goose
butter

Marinade

2 carrots and 2 onions, peeled and sliced
1 head celery, chopped
2 sliced lemons
1 sprig each parsley, thyme, marjoram
2 bay leaves
6 cloves
6 peppercorns
1 pint (600ml) olive oil
1/2 pint (300ml) white wine vinegar

Horseradish Sauce

1 root horseradish, peeled and grated
2 lemons, peeled and de-pipped
4 shallots, peeled and chopped
6 cloves
2 blades mace
1 teaspoon peppercorns
2 bay leaves
1 sprig thyme
½ pint (300ml) wine vinegar
1 lb (500g) redcurrant jelly
juice 2 oranges, Seville if possible

If these quantities appal you, cut them down by half; they were after all catering for the gross appetites of the Victorians. Place the goose in the marinade for 2 days, turning every so often.

Remove and dry, spread with butter, then wrap loosely in foil. Roast in a pre-heated oven at 375/Gas Mark 5/190C for 20 - 25 minutes to the lb (500g) (see previous recipe) until tender. The juice should run clear when the leg is pierced with a skewer. Transfer bird to a warmed serving dish. Cook all the sauce ingredients except the jelly and orange juice until it has reduced by half then add to the de-greased goose gravy. Reduce further to ¼ pint (150ml), add the jelly and orange juice, cook for 5 minutes then strain into a sauce boat.

Serve with plain boiled rice and an orange and chicory salad.

Brown Bread Cream

This delicious cream can be accompanied by any kind of fruit, and makes a nice light ending to a rich meal such as goose.

—————————— Serves 4 - 6 ——————————

2 egg yolks
½ pint (300ml) milk
1 stick cinnamon
1 - 2 tablespoons (15 - 30ml) sugar
0.04 oz (11g) sachet gelatine dissolved in 1
*   tablespoon (15ml) water (see p.163)*
2 oz (50g) fresh granary breadcrumbs
½ pint (300ml) crème fraîche
2 egg whites, stiffly whipped

Beat the egg yolks. Heat the milk with the cinnamon stick and pour onto the egg yolks. Return to the saucepan and cook over a very low heat, stirring constantly until the custard coats the back of a spoon. Sweeten to taste and leave to cool. Remove the cinnamon, add the gelatine and breadcrumbs and stir well. Fold in the crème fraîche and lastly the egg whites. Pour into an oiled 1½ pint (900ml) ring mould and refrigerate. Turn out and fill the centre of the brown bread cream with fruit.

SNIPE

Snipe are a great delicacy and now, owing to modern drainage schemes, becoming more of a rarity, though they still abound in certain natural habitats. The only snipe poaching story that I know concerns an episode in which Archie and I were unwittingly involved. We had taken tickets to fish the Teifi Pools (before they were dammed). The trout were not co-operative and the ghillie suggested that Archie might like to 'walk up' some snipe and then come back and try the fishing again in the evening. A great day was had on the Tregaron Marshes and neighbouring farms and Archie shot several snipe and one or two duck, and at the end of the day the ghillie was given a nice tip. Thirty-odd years later we were having supper with some friends and the talk got round to snipe shooting and this particular day. There was a deathly hush and then a loud guffaw of laughter from the other guest and it transpired that we had been poaching. Owen the ghillie was also the keeper on his estate and this was not the only time he had made his employer's game available. Some years after our visit the Earl had returned unexpectedly from a trip abroad and to his astonishment found the lawn in front of his stately pile covered with tents. It transpired that the said Owen had been making a good income out of letting the ground for camping and also the shooting. After a severe talking to, and premature retirement, he was allowed to stay on in his cottage until he died as he and his family had been in service on the estate for several generations.

Roast Snipe

As with woodcock, folklore has it that you should just let it pass through a hot oven but I think 15 – 20 minutes is just right. Being so small you can hardly make a meal off one snipe, so you need two per person if it is going to be a main course, or just use it as a savoury or bonne-bouche if you don't have many.

——————— Serves 2 - 4 ———————

4 snipe
4 chicken livers plus the snipe livers, chopped
*   and lightly sautéed*
melted butter
4 rounds of toast
1 tablespoon (15ml) good stock (see p.160)
1 squeeze of lemon juice
salt and pepper

Pre-heat the oven to 450F/Gas Mark 8/230C. Stuff the snipe with the chopped livers, season, place on the toast in a pan and baste with the butter. Cook for 15 – 20 minutes. Remove to a dish, swill out the pan with the stock and a squeeze of lemon juice, and pour over the birds. No accompaniment is needed for this gourmet game bird.

Danish Snipe Pie

I personally think it is a shame to do other than roast snipe, but if you want a change this is very delicious and also makes a few snipe go further.

―――――――――― *Serves 4 - 6* ――――――――――

2 shallots, peeled and very finely chopped
2 oz (50g) button mushrooms, finely sliced
1 oz (25g) butter
1 oz (25g) flour
½ pint (300ml) stock (see p.160) or stock cube
    and water
1 glass dry, white wine
6 snipe
1 lb (500g) pork sausagemeat
1 tablespoon (15ml) chopped parsley
2 oz (50g) onion, finely chopped
½ lemon, squeezed

Cook the shallots and mushrooms in the butter for a few seconds and then add the flour and finally the stock and wine and make a thin béchamel sauce. Stew the snipe very gently in this until tender, about 45 minutes. Mix remaining ingredients together and line a 1½ pint (900ml) pie dish with ⅔ of the resulting forcemeat. Split the snipe in two and lay on the forcemeat. Top up with the sauce in which they were cooked and cover with the remainder of the forcemeat. Bake in a pre-heated oven set at 400F/Gas Mark 6/200C for 45 minutes.

Serve with sprouts and chestnuts and mashed potatoes and any extra sauce.

Welsh Pudding

After spending a day 'walking up' snipe over marshy, tussocky terrain the hunters will be ready for a gargantuan meal and will feel their digestions can cope with a good rib-sticking pudding. This one seemed particularly appropriate as some of the best snipe shooting is to be found in Wales.

———————— *Serves 4 - 6* ————————

shortcrust pastry, using 6oz (75g) flour
  (see p.164)
12 oz (350g) jam
4 oz (125g) butter
4 oz (125g) sugar
1 teaspoon grated lemon rind
2 eggs
4 oz (125g) plain flour
½ teaspoon baking powder

Line a shallow 8" (20cm) dish or tin with the pastry and spread a thick layer of jam on the bottom. Cream the butter and sugar until light and fluffy and then add the egg and beat well. Stir in the lemon rind, sifted flour, salt and baking powder and spread over the jam. Pre-heat oven to 375F/Gas Mark 5/190C and bake for 30 minutes.

Serve hot or cold with crème fraîche or smetana.

WOODCOCK

Woodcock is much sought after both as a gourmet delicacy and as one of the most elusive and sporting game birds. They are migratory and their arrival depends very much on the weather, so you can never be absolutely sure that they will be in your neck of the woods when you want them. The only way of ensuring that you have enough for a dinner party is to freeze the odd one or two, as they are shot, until you have accumulated the number you require. There are still the occasional traditionalists who like to eat them with the 'trail' or innards but they are now the exception rather than the rule. You can augment the woodcock liver and heart with a couple of chicken livers and use this to squash up on the toast on which the bird has been roasted.

Terrine of Woodcock with Truffle

This is for a very special occasion, such as an anniversary, as you really have to lash out on the truffle. You could economise and use ceps but it wouldn't be quite the same.

———————— *Serves 4 - 6* ————————

2 woodcock
1 truffle
1 tablespoon (15ml) good brandy (don't economise and use a cheap brand)
8 oz (300g) chicken livers, plus the woodcock livers, trimmed
salt and pepper
1 pinch allspice
2 eggs, well beaten
thin slices of pork fat (hard back fat if possible)

Remove the breasts from the woodcock, slice very thinly, lay in a dish with the truffle, sprinkle with the brandy and marinate for 2 hours. Chop the rest of the woodcock flesh and livers very finely, or whizz in the food processor. Season with salt and pepper and a pinch of allspice. Add the brandy from the marinate and the two eggs. Line a ½ pint (300ml) terrine with pork fat and spoon in a layer of mixture, then the breast fillets and finally the rest of the mixture, placing more pork fat over the top. Cut the truffle into slices and lay them down the centre, and cover tightly with foil. Stand in a roasting tin and pour in boiling water to come half way up the side of the terrine. Place in a pre-heated oven set at 350F/Gas Mark 4/175C for 1 hour or until the juice comes out clear when you pierce it with a skewer. Cool and refrigerate for 2 - 3 days for the flavours to develop. Allow to come to room temperature for 1 hour before eating.

Serve with thin toast and, if possible, farmhouse butter.

Roast Woodcock

I am not a devotee of the school of thought which advocates that a woodcock or snipe should just fly through the oven. For my personal taste woodcock should be roasted at a high heat for 30 minutes, but if you prefer them less well done, cut the time down to 20 - 25 minutes.

———————————— *Serves 2* ————————————

2 woodcock
butter
2 woodcock livers, plus hearts, trimmed
2 chicken livers (or other game livers, if you have them), trimmed
2 thick slices bread, with crusts removed
2 rashers of bacon, de-rinded and fried
1 pinch nutmeg
salt and freshly ground black pepper
1 tablespoon (15ml) brandy

Pre-heat the oven to 450F/Gas Mark 7/220C and melt some butter in a small roasting pan. When it is foaming put in the woodcock, stuffed with the livers, and baste them well. Sit them on the toast and cover with the bacon. Cook for 20 – 30 minutes, depending on how rare you like them, then transfer to a warmed dish. Swill the pan out with the brandy and let it bubble for a few seconds. Remove the livers and mash them with the nutmeg, some salt and pepper. Chop the bacon, moisten with the brandy and pan juices and add to the mashed livers. Spread on the toast and sit the woodcock on top.

Serve with game chips and watercress salad.

Woodcock Lucullus

Another delicious way to serve woodcock for a dinner party, but you must be really organized as they should reach the table as soon as you have taken them from the grill.

—————— *Serves 2* ——————

2 woodcock
butter for roasting
4 oz (125g) button mushrooms
2 rounds of fried bread
orange juice
2 fl oz (60ml) single cream
1 egg yolk
breadcrumbs
salt and pepper

Pre-heat oven to 450F/Gas Mark 7/220C and roast the woodcock in the butter with the mushrooms. Have the fried bread ready on a flame proof dish, sit the woodcock on top and surround with the mushrooms. Pour over the cream, into which you have beaten the egg yolk. Sprinkle with breadcrumbs and flash under the grill for a few seconds until it crisps. Make gravy from the pan juices in which you have squeezed some orange juice.

Serve with plain boiled noodles and a green salad.

Old Fashioned Apple Charlotte

This is a good way of using up stale bread and any surplus apples. It should be turned out, but if you feel faint-hearted leave it in a straight-sided oven proof glass soufflé dish. It looks just as nice.

─────────────── *Serves 4 - 6* ───────────────

2 lbs (1 kg) cooking apples, peeled, cored and cut
  up
4 oz (125g) dark muscovado sugar
1 oz (25g) butter
rind of 1 lemon
1 tablespoon (15ml) water or lemon juice
8 - 10 slices of white bread with the crusts cut off
melted butter
4 tablespoons (60ml) demerara sugar,
  for the topping

Cook the apples with the sugar, butter, lemon rind and water, or lemon juice, until pulpy. Meanwhile dip the slices of bread in the melted butter and line the bottom and sides of a 2 pint (1 litre) dish with them. Spoon in the apple pulp and cover with a further layer of bread slices dipped in butter. Sprinkle with sugar and bake in a pre-heated oven at 350F/Gas Mark 4/175C for 1 hour.

Serve with cream or homemade custard.

Grilled Woodcock Breast Savoury

Savouries seem to have gone out of fashion these days, but before the war no dinner party would have been complete without a savoury at the end of a meal. Probably a relic of the days when the men sitting over their port was an essential part of the scene. As woodcock is rather rich this would be a good way to finish off a meal where the main course has been a light fish dish.

Serves 4

4 woodcock breasts
butter
4 squares of toast, spread with Gentleman's Relish
(or softened butter mixed with anchovy essence)

Fry the woodcock breasts in butter for 3 - 4 minutes on each side, then place on the squares of toast and serve immediately.

BLACKGAME

Blackgame is a blanket term which comprises red and black grouse, ptarmigan and capercailzie, the best known and most widely available being the red grouse which, from the culinary point of view, is also the most desirable. From a cook's point of view any recipe for red grouse will be suitable for ptarmigan. Capercailzie live on a diet of pine shoots so, when cooked, have an unmistakable taste of resin which makes them well nigh inedible, apart from the fact that they are now rather rare. Blackcock are tough even when young so, unless your hunter insists, try and avoid cooking them. If you have to, lengthy marinating and long and slow stewing or braising, with lots of flavouring is the answer. On the continent they are a prized quarry and hunters shoot the birds when their eyes are closed during the 'lek' or mating dance. This is the moment when they extend their wings, display their tails in a white fan and open their beaks to give an orgasmic territorial cry. I have always thought it decidedly unfair to shoot them at this moment and I know that Archie felt the same.

Roast Young Greyhen with Haggis Stuffing

Greyhen is the female of the blackcock, and provided your hunter has shot a young one, they can be quite delicious. This combination goes very well, as the haggis helps to make the flesh nice and moist and gives added flavour.

———————— *Serves 2* ————————

1 haggis
1 onion, peeled and chopped
1 teaspoon dried thyme
1 tablespoon (15ml) whisky
1 greyhen, plucked and drawn
2 rashers bacon, de-rinded
2 oz (50g) butter
salt and pepper
¼ pint (150ml) stock (see p.160), or water
    and stock cube
1 teaspoon rowan jelly
1 teaspoon balsamic vinegar
1 slice toast

Remove the filling from the haggis and mix with the onion, thyme, and whisky and spoon into the body cavity of the greyhen. Pre-heat the oven and set at 350F/Gas Mark 4/175C and melt the butter in a roasting pan until foaming. Cover the bird with the bacon rashers and season well. Place on the toast in the pan, baste well and roast for 1 – 1½ hours, basting frequently. Remove the greyhen to a heated dish and degrease the pan. Add the stock, jelly and vinegar and bubble fiercely on top of the stove until it looks syrupy, then pour into a sauce boat.

Serve with ribbon potatoes or 'Skirlie Mirlie'. To make the ribbon potatoes, cut peeled potatoes in thin ribbons like orange peel and fry in deep fat.

'Skirlie Mirlie'

This goes well with any kind of roast game.

———————— *Serves 2* ————————

1 lb (500g) cooked potato
1 lb (500g) cooked turnip, swede or parsnip
1 oz (25g) butter
milk
salt and pepper
croûtons of fried bread

Combine the potato, turnip, butter and milk in a saucepan and beat well until light and creamy. Season well and transfer to a hot dish. Sprinkle with the croûtons.

Honeycomb Cream

This delicious, airy pudding goes very well with fresh raspberries or strawberries and makes a light ending after the rich greyhen.

———————— *Serves 4 - 6* ————————

1½ pints (900ml) milk
sugar to taste
2 x 0.04oz (11g) sachets gelatine
1 vanilla pod
3 eggs

Soak the gelatine in a little milk in a bowl until soft. Add the sugar, remaining milk and vanilla pod and stand the bowl in a saucepan of hot water. Heat until the gelatine is dissolved, stirring constantly. Beat the egg yolks and whisk them slowly and carefully into the hot milk mixture until the custard has thickened, stirring constantly. Take the pan off the heat and cool. Fold in the stiffly beaten egg whites. When the mixture is nearly cold, pour into an oiled 2 pint (1 litre) mould or pudding basin. Refrigerate and turn out when needed.

PIGEON

When Archie was instructing at the RMA at Sandhurst at the end of the war he used to escape the pressures of military life by shooting pigeons. The going rate for a pigeon in the feather in those days was 2/6d (12½p). I think the seed of an idea to become a professional pigeon shooter must have germinated then, lying dormant until the year after we married. That summer every weekend was spent pigeon shooting in Hampshire, camping out. We had no tent and if it rained had to retire to a cattle shed where I used to have to make a fire on ground strewn with dried cattle dung, so on these occasions Archie christened me the 'Yak Woman'! Then the momentous decision was taken to turn professional. Money was in short supply and to begin with we lived in a local pub called the Deane Gate Inn, and to help pay for our board and lodging we used to wash up the glasses after closing time. The petrol for any holiday or visit had to be paid for by pigeons shot, and the last day was invariably spent in a pigeon hide on some strange farm on the way back where Archie had talked the owner into letting him shoot. The journey home was pretty chilly as the birds were laid out to cool in the back of the car with all the windows left open, and Lucy as a child was bedded down on the back seat. The upshot of all this meant that many thousands of pigeons passed through our hands and I experimented with countless ways of cooking them, writing about it as often as possible in the hope of persuading the great British housewife to cook this delicious bird. Over the centuries pigeon has certainly made a welcome change of diet for many country dwellers and was considered quite a delicacy.

Pigeon Pâté with Cider

Over the years I have experimented with different kinds of pigeon pâté and have come to the conclusion that they lend themselves to almost any combination. This makes a light and delicate pâté.

—————————— *Serves 6 - 8* ——————————

6 oz (175g) butter
2 shallots, peeled and finely chopped
4 oz (125g) apple, peeled and chopped
8 pigeon breasts, skinned and cut into small dice
1 teaspoon apple jelly
1 teaspoon mild Dijon mustard
1 pinch of dried thyme and rosemary
salt and ground black pepper
¼ pint (150ml) cider
1 tablespoon (15ml) cream
1 tablespoon (15ml) fromage frais
melted butter, or aspic jelly made with cider, to cover.
blanched apple slices to decorate

Melt the butter until foaming and cook the shallot and apple, then tip in the diced pigeon and sauté until cooked but still pink inside. Remove from the pan with a slotted spoon and transfer to the food processor and whizz until finely ground. Add the jelly, mustard, herbs and seasoning to the pan then pour in the cider and allow to bubble for a few seconds, finally stir in the cream and fromage frais. Switch on the food processor and tip the liquid in through the top and blend until really smooth. Taste and adjust seasoning then spoon into a 1 pint (600ml) terrine. Allow to cool and then cover with either melted butter or, if you are going to eat it within a day or two, pour on a covering of aspic jelly made with cider. Decorate with slices of apple blanched in boiling water for a few seconds.

Pigeon Breast with Ginger, Lemon and Honey

This is a party recipe and is equally good hot or cold. I would almost go so far as to say that it is *nouvelle cuisine*.

————————— *Serves 4* —————————

8 pigeon breasts
butter for frying
4 tablespoons (60ml) ginger and honey juice
juice of ½ a lemon

Ginger and Honey Sauce

4 oz (125g) stem ginger
3oz (75g) sugar
¼ pint (150ml) water
2 tablespoons (60ml) runny honey

To make the sauce, pulverise the ginger in your food processor or liquidizer. Dissolve the sugar in the water and boil, without stirring, for 4 minutes. Add the honey to the ginger then switch on the processor and pour the syrup in through the top and whizz until it is as smooth as you can get it. Put into a warmed jar and, when cool, refrigerate. To cook the pigeon heat the butter until foaming in a wok or large frying pan and sautée the pigeon breasts for 3 minutes on each side. Slosh in the ginger sauce and cook for a few seconds more, shaking well. Remove breasts to a plate. Add lemon juice and cook the sauce until it is thick and syrupy. Take a very sharp knife and slice breasts very thinly lengthways but do not sever completely. Press out into a fan shape and lay on a dish or on individual plates. Dribble the sauce over each one.

Serve with a parsnip purée, to which you have added a pinch of turmeric and a squeeze of orange juice, and pommes parisienne. If they are to be eaten cold, garnish with thinly sliced fennel with lemon and oil dressing, and sprinkle with toasted pine nuts.

Bachelor's Pigeon

Graham Harvey Evers, who used to run Gaybird game farm gave me this recipe which he dreamed up before he got married. It had the added attraction that he could leave it simmering away on the stove while he went out to deal with his incubators and chicks. I have always suspected that he shot some pigeons, decided to cook them, found some onions and an open bottle of red wine and chucked them all in a saucepan together, and as an afterthought tipped in the remains of a packet of raisins! It is a jolly good winter warmer.

——————————— *Serves 2* ———————————

2 oven-ready pigeons
1 lb (500g) peeled onions, sliced in thick rings
4 oz (125g) raisins
2 teaspoons demerara sugar
1 bottle cheap red wine
salt and pepper
1 rounded teaspoon cornflour
gravy browning

Put the pigeons on top of a layer of onions in the bottom of a saucepan, cover with the rest of the onion rings and the raisins. Add the sugar, red wine, salt and plenty of pepper. Cover tightly and simmer gently for 1½ - 2 hours, or until the pigeons are tender. Remove them to a serving dish, fish out the onion rings and arrange round the birds. Reduce the liquid to ½ pint (300ml), add the cornflour mixed with a little water and a drop or two of gravy browning and stir until it thickens, then pour over the pigeons.

Mashed potato is all you need to go with it, to mop up the gravy.

Braised Pigeon stuffed with Sweetcorn and Apple

At the end of January, before the spring drilling starts, pigeon go mad for maize strips which have been planted for the pheasants and, unusually for them, develop strips of fat over the breast so that they resemble the corn-fed chickens you see on the supermarket shelves. For those of you lucky enough to live in an area where these strips have been planted try and get your hands on some of these birds. Failing this just use run-of-the-mill pigeons. This casserole can be cooked ahead of time and re-heated.

Serves 2

1 shallot, peeled and finely chopped
¼ apple, peeled and finely chopped
2 oz (50g) butter
1 rasher bacon, finely chopped and fried
* until crisp*
1 oz (25g) fresh white breadcrumbs
3 oz (75g) tinned whole corn kernels
½ teaspoon dried sage
¼ pint (150ml) cider
salt and pepper

Sauté the shallot and apple in a little of the butter until soft then mix with the bacon, breadcrumbs, sweet corn and seasonings and stuff the pigeons with it. Melt the rest of the butter in a casserole and brown the pigeons in it. Add the cider, cover tightly, and place in a pre-heated oven at 325F/Gas Mark 3/160C for 2½ - 3 hours or until tender.

Serve with calabrese or chopped curly kale and new potatoes.

Wokked Pigeon

This is a 'quickie' which can be cooked in a wok, frying pan or under the grill and solves the question of what to give the unexpected guest or your hunter/partner who adopts a cave man attitude and demands an instant meal from his trophies. He may also have brought you some Oyster Mushrooms *Pleurotus ostreatus,* those satiny grey mushrooms which grow on old deciduous tree stumps, particularly beech. If not, they are now commercially grown.

———————— *Serves 2 - 4* ————————

8 pigeon breasts
butter for frying
4 oz (125g) oyster mushrooms (or fresh or tinned
*   ordinary mushrooms) finely sliced*
1 teaspoon redcurrant jelly
2 or 3 good shakes soy sauce
1 shake Lea & Perrins Worcestershire Sauce
salt and pepper
¼ pint (150ml) single cream, or half cream and
*   half Greek yoghurt*

Cut the pigeon breasts into thin strips lengthways. Heat the butter until foaming and throw in the pigeon strips and cook for a few seconds, stirring furiously. Add all the other ingredients, except the cream, cook for a few seconds more and then add the cream. Scrape all the nice brown bits off the pan and serve with rice or on pieces of thick, buttered toast. Sleight of hand, dexterity and speed are of the essence as the pigeon strips should still be faintly pink inside.

Pigeon and Guinness Casserole

This is my British answer to the traditional Flemish peasant dish *Carbonnade* - a casserole of meat made with beer. I have used Guinness as I think it goes so well with the dark meat of the pigeon, but you can use a dark ale if you wish. It freezes well and is best made the day before and then re-heated.

―――――――――――― *Serves 6 - 8* ――――――――――――

16 pigeon breasts cut into chunks
4 oz (125g) fat bacon
2 oz (50g) butter or lard
10 shallots, peeled and left whole
4 carrots, peeled and cut into thick rounds
2 oz (50g) flour
½ pint (300ml) Guinness or dark ale
¼ pint (150ml) stock, or stock cube and water
1 tablespoon (15ml) dark muscovado brown
    sugar
2 teaspoons concentrated tomato purée
salt and pepper
1 dash red wine vinegar
1 teaspoon redcurrant jelly (optional)

Brown the pigeon breasts and bacon in the fat, then add the vegetables and cook for a few minutes. Sprinkle in the flour and add the Guinness, stock and all the other ingredients except the wine vinegar and redcurrant jelly. Tip into a 3 pint (1.8 litre) casserole and cook in a pre-heated oven set at 400F/Gas Mark 6/200C for 15 minutes and then turn down to 325F/Gas Mark 3/160C for 2 - 3 hours. Add a dash of vinegar and taste to see if it requires the jelly. If you want to make this into a carbonnade, cover the top with slices of French bread spread with mustard, baste with the pigeon liquid and place under a grill until it browns.

You need a good mopper-up for the rich sauce, so an alternative to mashed potato would be pease pudding. Spring greens or savoy cabbage quickly cooked, and then processed for a few quick short bursts in the food processor, goes well, too.

Pigeon Cobbler

I like to think that my latest concoction follows in the tradition of cottage cookery. My home tasting panel thought it was a winner.

—————————— *Serves 4 - 6* ——————————

10 pigeon breasts
2 oz (50g) flour, seasoned with salt, pepper and
*   mixed herbs*
1 large onion, peeled and sliced
4 oz (125g) button mushrooms
½ pint (300ml) stock (see p.160) or stock cube
*   and water*
2 bay leaves
6 streaky bacon rashers, rolled and fastened
*   with cocktail sticks*
3 hard boiled eggs, cut into quarters
potato or cornflour (optional)
1 tablespoon chopped parsley
cheese cobbler topping, made with 4 oz (125g)
*   flour (see p.166)*

Roll the pigeon breasts and onion in the flour, place in a casserole with the mushrooms, sprinkle in the remainder of the flour, pour in the stock and lay the bay leaves and bacon rolls on top. Cover and place in a pre-heated oven at 400F/Gas Mark 6/200C for 15 minutes and then turn down to 325F/Gas Mark 3/150C for 2 hours or until tender. Take out of the oven and remove the cocktail sticks from the bacon rolls and dot them and the quartered eggs over the top of the pigeon. If the juice looks too thin thicken with a little potato or cornflour. Allow to cool a little and sprinkle on the chopped parsley. Roll out cheese cobbler topping to ½" (1cm) thick and cut out 2" (5cm) circles. Lay these in overlapping rows over the pigeon and place in a pre-heated oven set at 400F/Gas Mark 6/200C for 20 - 30 minutes or until risen and golden.

Pease Pudding

This was a staple main course in the old days and my daughter Lucy's old nanny Frankie often made it for her family. It is also good when cold cut into slices and fried for breakfast. Good calorific stuff for a returning wildfowler or pigeon shooter who thinks he has just avoided hypothermia.

———————— *Serves 4* ————————

8 oz (250g) split yellow peas
1 onion, peeled and chopped
stock, preferably ham or a ham stock cube
 dissolved in hot water
1 egg, beaten
1 oz (25g) butter
salt and freshly ground black pepper

Soak the peas for 12 hours and then drain. Put into a pan with the onion and enough stock to cover and cook over a low heat with the lid on until tender, adding more stock if necessary. Whizz in the food processor and then add the egg and butter. Check seasoning and spoon into a 8" (20cm) greased cake tin and cover with buttered foil. Cook in a pre-heated oven at 325F/Gas Mark 3/160C for 30 - 40 minutes.

Rhubarb Gingerbread Pudding

In spring in times past, and even today you would always notice an upturned bucket or two at the end of any cottage vegetable garden. Its function was to blanch the young rhubarb and protect the delicate rose pink shoots from frost. The first pickings should be cooked over a low heat with little or no water, sweetened with demerara sugar and served with cream or Greek yoghurt. Later on when the sticks become coarser this is a good way to use them and makes a filling family pudding. The gingerbread mixture goes particularly well, as rhubarb has a special affinity with ginger.

———————————— *Serves 4 - 6* ————————————

3 oz (90g) treacle
2 oz (50g) butter
1 heaped teaspoon ground ginger
1 level teaspoon ground cinnamon
¼ pint (150ml) milk
1 heaped teaspoon bicarbonate of soda
8 oz (300g) plain flour
1 egg, well beaten
6 sticks rhubarb, chopped into 1" (2 cm) pieces
2 oz (50g) sugar

Put the treacle, butter, ginger and cinnamon in a pan and melt over a low heat and then add the milk. Heat to blood heat and stir in the bicarbonate of soda. Pour into a mixing bowl and sift in the flour, beating with a whisk or electric beaters. Finally beat in the egg. Pour half this mixture into a buttered 1½ pint (900ml) fireproof dish, scatter the rhubarb and sugar over it and then pour over the remainder. Pre-heat the oven and set at 350F/Gas Mark 4/175C and cook for 45 minutes to 1 hour

Serve with custard, cream or yoghurt.

Homemade Cider

In times gone by, owing to lack of money and transport, nearly every cottage or farmhouse made some kind of alcoholic drink. I can remember sampling some pretty strange and potent brews when we went in to see keeper friends after a day's pigeon shooting. Before the days of freezers it really was a way of using up some of the garden glut. Parsnip and runner bean were two I remember with particular aversion, but out of politeness had to smack my lips with seeming enjoyment. This is a good way of using up windfall or crab apples.

windfall apples, neither peeled nor cored
water
1¼ lbs (550g) sugar per gallon of liquid

Wash the apples, cut them up and put them into a clean plastic bucket, which has been sterilised with Campden tablets. Cover with water and put a clean tea towel over the top to protect from dust. Let it stand for about 10 days giving it a daily stir. When fermentation has ceased, strain it and add the appropriate amount of sugar per gallon. Pour into sterilised bottles and let it stand uncorked for 14 days. Cork securely (but don't use screw tops) and leave for 3 months, at the end of which time you should have clear, sparkling cider.

ROOK

Rook is rarely available and is unlikely to be seen on your local supermarket shelves, but when I first came to live in this village, forty years ago, older locals would have eaten their annual feast of rook pie in mid-May as this was the traditional time for the cull of fledgelings. It would have made a welcome change of diet for Lucy's old nanny Frankie for, as I have said previously, money was tight and anything in the way of nature's freebie was seized upon avidly. During the war, when meat was rationed, rooks fetched the unimaginable sum of 2/9d each.

May 8th to 18th is the traditional period during which 'branchers' are shot. This is when young rooks emerge from the nest but have not yet flown. Young Victorian virgins used to sally forth armed with rook rifles and shoot them, it being apparently deemed a suitably ladylike pursuit.

Mrs Munday's Rook Pie

In my search for an authentic recipe I visited the Gamekeepers Inn at Mapledurwell, as my spies had told me that they served an incomparable pie. Unfortunately the proprietor's mother, who had made these pies, died three years ago, taking the recipe with her. However, Mr Munday kindly recreated it for me, so I can vouch for the fact that it really is as delicious as my spies had told me. Here is the recipe.

―――――――――― *Serves 4 - 6* ――――――――――

1 pig's trotter, split
2 onions, peeled and chopped
1 carrot
breasts from 8 rooks, plus legs and thighs
2 oz (50g) bacon, cut in chunks
salt and pepper
2 pints (1 litre) water, or more if necessary
1 tablespoon (15ml) parsley, chopped
shortcrust pastry, using 6 oz (75g) flour
 (see p.164)
1 egg, beaten

Place the pig's trotter, onions, carrot, rook breasts, legs and thighs, and bacon chunks in a saucepan. Season well and cover with the water. Bring slowly to the boil, then turn down the heat and simmer for 30 minutes. Remove the rook breasts, joints and bacon to a dish and let the stock simmer for a further hour. Lay the breasts and bacon chunks in a 2 pint (1 litre) pie dish and add the flesh from the legs and thighs. Strain the stock, adjust the seasoning, and pour it over the meat to come within 1" (2cm) of the top. Sprinkle the parsley over it and cool. When cold, cover with shortcrust pastry, make a hole in the top, decorate with pastry leaves and brush with beaten egg. Place in a pre-heated oven set at 425F/Gas Mark 7/220C for 1 hour. Make a paper funnel and pour in extra jellied stock.

Rook Lyonnaise

As a change from the more mundane pie or pudding here is a French recipe which is very good, albeit fattening.

———————— *Serves 2 - 4* ————————

8 rook breasts
milk
flour for coating
1 egg, beaten
breadcrumbs
olive oil for frying
2 large onions, peeled and cut into thick rings
sherry vinegar

Soak the breasts overnight in milk. Drain and dry them, then coat in flour, dip in egg and then in breadcrumbs. Heat the olive oil and fry the onion rings until crisp and brown then drain on kitchen paper. Wipe the frying pan with paper and pour in more oil. When hot, fry the rook breasts for about 4 minutes on each side or until golden. Mound the onion rings in the centre of a dish and arrange the breasts in a circle around it. Drain off the oil, swill out with a few drops of sherry vinegar and pour over the rooks.

Serve with lightly cooked purple sprouting broccoli.

Gooseberry and Elderflower Mousse

Before the advent of gardening programmes on television and the widespread growth of garden centres, with all the modern aids to pest control, every cottage garden would have a few fruit bushes, gooseberry, red and black currant. Not for them the nylon netting to prevent the birds getting the fruit, instead each bush would be wrapped in an old net or lace curtain. Gooseberries would be made into pies, jams and jellies and were often flavoured with elderflower, a combination which I think is positively ambrosial. The following is a delicious recipe and, of course, now that we are lucky enough to be able to freeze our elderflower-flavoured gooseberry, we can bring back the memories of summer, at will.

—————————— *Serves 6 - 8* ——————————

1 lb (500g) gooseberries, topped and tailed
sugar to taste
2 heads of elderflower
3 egg yolks
3 egg whites, stiffly beaten
0.04 oz (11g) sachet gelatine (see p.163)
½ pint (300ml) cream whipped to soft peaks

Top and tail the gooseberries, rinse and drain. Tip into a saucepan with the sugar. Cook over a low heat until soft then lay the elderflowers on top. Cover and leave for 10 minutes to infuse. Remove flowers and re-heat then spoon them into the food processor. Switch on, pour in the egg yolks while it is whizzing, to make a thick and creamy purée. Transfer to a bowl, allow to cool, then add the dissolved gelatine and stir well. Fold in the whipped cream and lastly the beaten egg whites and spoon into a 2 pint (1 litre) soufflé dish. Leave to set.

Gooseberry Fool

Omit the eggs and gelatine, and just fold in the whipped cream.

MIXED GAME

The recipes in the following chapter all contain more than one species of game, such as in Game Pie and appropriately Poacher's Stew. Nocturnal poaching expeditions no doubt yielded a mixed bag from pheasant to rabbit, pigeon, or partridge and if there was a large family to feed it all went into the one pot with whatever wild herbs were available.

Game Terrine

The following comes from Lady Ellesmere's book of recipes. The date is 1920. Her daughter says it was made in a deep French terrine dish. The instructions, as was so often the case in those days, are sketchy to say the least, so I had to work out my own version.

─────────── *Serves 6 - 8* ───────────

1 pheasant
1 hare
8-10 streaky rashers of smoked bacon,
    de-rinded
6 oz (175g) fresh breadcrumbs
hare and pheasant livers sautéed lightly and
    finely chopped
2 oz (50g) butter
2 eggs
4 tablespoons (60ml) milk
2 teaspoons mixed herbs
salt and pepper
1 pint (500ml) approximately, light game
    stock, strained (see p.160)

Cut the meat from the game and slice as thinly as possible. Line a 2 pint (1 litre) terrine with bacon rashers and make a well seasoned forcemeat with the breadcrumbs, livers, butter, eggs, milk, herbs and seasoning. Make alternate layers of forcemeat and game slices (light and dark mixed) and moisten with 5 tablespoons (75ml) light game stock. Cover tightly with foil and the lid. Stand the terrine in a roasting pan and half fill the pan with boiling water. Bake in a pre-heated oven set at 350F/Gas Mark 4/175C for 1½ - 2 hours or until the meat is tender. Meanwhile make a well-flavoured stock with the bones, then strain it and reduce it to about ½ pint (300ml). When the terrine is cooked, take it out of the oven, let it cool a little, put a weight on it and leave for 12 hours. Cover with a clear meat jelly. Make this by adding 0.04 oz (11g) gelatine to the warm stock (see p.163).

Serve with red whortleberry jelly.

Raised Game Pie

This is a good way to use up odd bits of game in your freezer which would not be enough on their own to feed weekend guests.

———————— *Serves 8 - 10* ————————

8 oz (250g) fat pork, minced
8 oz (250g) rabbit and pheasant meat, finely
   chopped
8 oz (250g) venison from fore-quarter or neck,
   finely chopped
4 oz (125g) pork sausagemeat
4 oz (125g) cooked ham, cut into small dice
1 shallot, peeled and finely chopped
1 teaspoon redcurrant jelly
1 pinch ground allspice
1 pinch ground bay leaves
salt and ground black pepper
½ pint (300ml) rich reduced game stock
   (see p.160)
0.04 oz (11g) gelatine (see p.163)
1 tablespoon (15ml) Madeira
hot water crust, made with 12oz (350g) flour
   (see p.164)

Mix together all the meats, shallot, jelly, seasonings and 2 table-spoons (30ml) of the stock. Cut off ⅓ of the pastry, cover and keep warm. Use the rest to line a loose-bottomed 8" (20cm) cake tin. Spoon in the meat filling. Brush the edges of the pastry with beaten egg. Roll out the remaining ⅓ of the pastry and cover the pie, sealing the edges firmly with a fork or your thumb. Cut a hole in the top of the pie and insert a small cardboard funnel. Decorate with pastry leaves and glaze with the rest of the beaten egg. Bake in a pre-heated oven set at 400F/Gas Mark 6/200C for 30 min-utes then turn down the heat to 350F/Gas Mark 4/180C for 1 hour. Cover the top with greaseproof paper if it is browning too much. Allow to cool slightly. Dissolve the gelatine in the Madeira, (see p.163) add to the remaining warm stock, cool until it is just beginning to thicken and pour through the paper funnel which you can then remove. Eat when cold, but try and take it out of the refrigerator at least 1½ hours before you are going to eat it, as there is nothing quite so nasty as pie straight out of the fridge.

Poacher's Stew

This is a winter warmer and is a meal in itself. You can please yourself what you put into it, so it is another good idea for when you are doing your annual deep freeze dredge and de-frost and find some of those unidentified corpses which you forgot to label, lurking in the depths.

——————————— *Serves 6 - 8* ———————————

1 rabbit, cut into joints
1 squirrel (if you have the nerve!), jointed
1 pheasant (perhaps a damaged one), cut into
    joints
8 oz (250g) green bacon in the piece
2 large onions, peeled and cut in chunks
1 small swede, peeled and cubed
1 lb (500g) potatoes peeled and halved
salt and pepper
water
1 tablespoon (15ml) each of wild garlic and
    sorrel, roughly chopped
1 handful young nettle tops
1 French stick, cut into slices 1" (2cm) thick
8 oz (250g) grated Cheddar cheese

Put the first 8 ingredients into a large saucepan with water to cover. Put on the lid, bring to the boil and simmer very slowly for about 2 hours, or until everything is very tender. At the last minute throw in the herbs and cook for 2 - 3 minutes longer. Tip into an ovenproof dish. Cover with overlapping slices of bread, sprinkle thickly with the grated cheese and brown under the grill.

Wash down with homemade beer, or wine if you prefer.

Hot Game Pie

Any kind of mixture will do, and if you haven't got enough game you can make up the difference with turkey or chicken breasts.

─────────── *Serves 6 - 8* ───────────

2 ½ lbs (1.25kg) raw game meat cut into 1"
(2cm) cubes. (1 hare, 1 pheasant, 1 pigeon
should render this amount of meat)
1 onion, peeled and chopped
4 oz (125g) oyster mushrooms, chanterelles or
cultivated mushrooms, unpeeled but wiped
with a piece of damp kitchen paper
2 teaspoons rowan jelly
2 fl oz (75ml) red wine
½ pint (300ml) stock (see p.160) or stock cube
and water
salt and pepper
beurre manié (see p.167)
shortcrust pastry, made with 12 oz (350g) flour
(see p.164)

Coat the joints with flour and put them into a casserole with the onion, jelly, wine, stock, salt and pepper. Cover and place in a pre-heated oven at 400F/Gas Mark 6/200C for 15 minutes, then turn heat down to 300F/Gas Mark 3/160C for 2½ - 3 hours or until tender. 15 minutes before the end of the cooking time stir in small lumps of beurre manié (see p.167) to thicken, and add more salt and pepper if required. Allow to cool, then arrange in a 2½ pint (1.4 litre) pie dish, strewn, with the whole mushrooms. Cover with the pastry and paint with beaten egg. Bake in a pre-heated oven set at 400F/Gas Mark 6/200C for 35 - 40 minutes, until golden.

Serve with new potatoes tossed in butter and, at the very last minute, a handful of dry oatmeal sprinkled on top. This potato recipe was invented by George Parker, a cousin of Archie's. A purée of swede flavoured with cinnamon complements it well.

Red Whortleberry Jelly

This pre-supposes that you know where you can pick 'worts'. If not, use cranberries or bilberries.
Makes 2 - 3 x 1lb (500g) pots.

2 pints (1 litre) 'worts' or cranberries
red wine
½ teaspoon ground cinnamon

Moisten the sugar with the red wine and cook until the sugar has dissolved. Add the fruit and cinnamon and cook until smooth, stirring constantly. Spoon into heated pots and cover.

Poivrade Sauce for Cold Game

This is another of Lady Durham's recipes and is dated 1900. It goes well with cold game.

———————————— *Serves 4 - 6* ————————————

2 shallots, finely chopped
2 tablespoons (30 ml) tarragon, basil, thyme,
*   sage and marjoram, finely chopped*
2 tablespoons (30 ml) parsley and mint, finely
*   chopped*
3 tablespoons (45 ml) tarragon vinegar
3 tablespoons (45 ml) olive oil
1 dash mushroom ketchup or Worcestershire
*   sauce*
sugar, to taste (my addition to the original
*   recipe)*
salt and pepper to taste

The original recipe, like so many of that era, specified Harvey's sauce which is, alas, no longer available. Mushroom ketchup or Worcestershire sauce make an acceptable substitute. Mix all together and serve in a sauceboat.

Raspberry Gratinée

I first tasted this pudding in a tiny little country restaurant right off the beaten track on one of my visits to France and it was so good that I asked Madame for the recipe. The raspberries were from her garden and the eggs from her chickens. She used *Biscottes,* which you can get in supermarkets here under the name of French Toasts, but I think you could equally well use trifle sponges. It is best made the previous day and should be served really cold.

———————— *Serves 4 - 6* ————————

1 pint (600ml) milk
2 - 3 tablespoons (30 - 45ml) sugar
1 stick cinnamon
1½lb (750g) raspberries
4 oz (125g) sugar
butter
4 eggs, well beaten
18 French Toasts
caster sugar for the topping
whole raspberries to decorate

Bring the milk to the boil with the sugar and the cinnamon stick, set aside and leave to infuse. Simmer the raspberries and the remaining sugar over a low heat until the juice runs, it won't take long. Butter a shallow 2½ pint (1.4 litre) square or oblong oven proof dish. Mine measures 12" (30cm) x 8½" (22cm) x 2" (5cm). Put in a layer of French Toasts, then cover this with the cooked raspberry and top up with a final layer of Toasts. Remove the cinnamon and pour the milk gradually onto the eggs, whisking constantly. Pour the custard mixture little by little over the toasts, waiting 10 minutes between additions so that they swell up. Leave the dish to stand for 15 minutes then bake in a preheated oven set at 350F/Gas Mark 4/175C for 30 - 40 minutes. When the pudding is cooked and golden cover it thickly with sugar. Flash under the grill to caramelise the topping and allow to cool. Before serving decorate with whole raspberries.

Homemade Beer

People are astonished at the amount of beer which is consumed nowadays but few can compare with the uncle of a friend of mine who, before the war, used to drink 10 pints daily. His poor wife brewed it in the copper every week after she had done the weekly wash. The mind boggles at the amount he must have consumed in his lifetime, but I gather he did not make old bones. Perhaps there is a moral there somewhere!

Makes 2 gallons (10 litres), approximately 18 x 1 pint (600ml) bottles.

1½ oz (40g) dried hops
1 oz (25g) black patent malt
Campden tablets,
water
1½ lb (750kg) dried malt extract
1 lb (500g) sugar
½ pkt beer yeast
extra priming sugar

Tie hops and black patent malt in a muslin bag and drop into a large saucepan of water, at least 5 pints (2.25 litres), and bring to the boil. Reduce the heat and simmer for 30 minutes. Meanwhile sterilize the bucket and bottles with a solution of Campden tablets and water as per the instructions on the bottle. Place malt extract and sugar in a 3 gallon (10.5 litre) sterilised plastic bucket, pour over a kettle of boiling water and stir to dissolve. Add hop liquid and top up with cold water. When the mixture is luke-warm add the yeast. Cover and leave for 7 days. Have ready 18 sterilised pint (600ml) bottles and into each one put 1 teaspoon sugar. Syphon beer into bottles, leaving 1" (2cm) airspace and seal with crown corks. In three weeks it should be crystal clear and ready to drink, but be careful when pouring to leave the sediment in the bottle.

HARE

The owner of a small, rough shoot in the Midlands had been troubled by a gang of poachers 'lamping' for hares at night with their long dogs. A friend of his happened to call in one day to see him at his office. When he walked in he saw, to his amazement, that the entire top of the desk was covered with cement models of hares, such as you would find in a garden centre. When he asked the reason for this strange assembly, his friend said that he was sticking on reflective eyes and planned to dot them about in the fields known to be frequented by the gang, so that when they saw the shining eyes in the light of the torch they would be gulled into thinking they were the real McCoy. On being asked what good it would do, he said he reckoned it would give the poachers a bit of a fright and when they discovered the joke they would look pretty silly. Anyway, he added, it was going to make him feel one hell of a lot better, even if it didn't stop them.

Roast Baron of Hare

Mention hare and it evokes strong reactions as people either love it or loathe it (or the thought thereof). I think it is all those recipes which say 'keep the blood to thicken the stew'. Well, unless you are hell-bent on being a traditionalist, it is quite unnecessary and you can get just as rich a flavour by other means. Hare is now widely available in supermarkets so you don't have to tackle the rather 'yukky' process of cleaning and skinning which some of us have had to face in the past (as a result of the squeamishness of our loved ones).

A hare weighs anything from 5lbs (2 kg) to 7lbs (3.2 kg). A baron of hare consists of the saddle and hind legs. The forequarters can be used in other recipes.

———————— *Serves 4* ————————

1 baron of young hare weighing approximately
4½- 5 lbs (2 kg - 2.25 kg)
brown muscovado sugar
1 pinch each allspice and ground ginger
2 sprigs parsley
1 onion, peeled and finely chopped
4 oz (125g) butter, melted
2 glasses port
½ pint (300ml) stock (see p. 160)
2 teaspoons red wine vinegar
1 tablespoon (15ml) rowan jelly
salt and pepper

Remove the white skin and tissue from the saddle and hindquarters of the hare and rub all over with the sugar and spices. Leave for 3 hours, longer if possible. Lay the hare on top of the parsley and onion in a roasting dish, season, pour over the melted butter and lay a piece of foil on top. Pre-heat the oven to 375F/Gas Mark 5/190C and bake the hare for 1 hour. Remove the foil, pour over the port and cook for a further 15 minutes, then transfer to a serving dish. Pour in the stock, rowan jelly and vinegar and stir well to incorporate all the brown bits, adjust seasoning and strain into a gravy boat.

Serve with braised chicory and croquette potatoes.

Medallions of Hare in a Cream Sauce

This is a quick and easy dish which does not need a lot of complicated preparation and, provided the hare is young, little or no marinating is needed.

——————— *Serves 4* ———————

*2 fillets of hare weighing approximately 1 lb
   (500g)
1 tablespoon best olive oil
1 clove garlic, peeled and finely chopped
butter for sautéeing
1 squeeze lemon juice
1 teaspoon sloe and apple jelly
1 small pinch cayenne pepper
salt and ground black pepper
1 tablespoon (15ml) crème fraîche*

Remove the white skin and membrane and cut each fillet diagonally into four. Flatten with the heel of your hand, smear each side with oil and sprinkle with garlic. Cover with clingfilm and leave for ½ an hour, or longer if you wish. Heat the butter in a thick pan until foaming, blot the oil off the medallions with kitchen paper and sauté for 2 minutes on each side - they should still be pink in the middle. Remove to a dish. Add the lemon juice, jelly and seasonings and finally the crème fraîche. Spoon a little over each of the medallions.

Garnish with triangles of fried bread and shaggy inkcap mushrooms. Serve with matchstick potatoes and steamed, diced, celeriac.

Italian Hare Stew

This stew is suitable for the old stager and if you have an Aga it can be left in the low oven overnight. The contrast of sour and sweet offsets the richness of the hare. This is definitely one of those dishes that pay for re-heating. It freezes well.

─────────────── *Serves 8 - 10* ───────────────

1 hare weighing approximately 7 lbs (3.2 kg)
1 bottle red wine
2 pints (1 litre) water
1 whole onion, peeled and stuck with cloves
2 carrots
1 stick celery
¼ pint (150ml) olive oil
2 oz (50g) stoned raisins
1 oz (25g) walnuts
1 oz (25g) muscovado sugar
2 bay leaves
1 sprig rosemary
1 cinnamon stick, or 1 pinch ground cinnamon
peel from 1 orange, cut into julienne strips, and
    the juice
salt and ground black pepper
beurre manié (see p.167)

Remove the meat from the bones and cut into chunks. Make a stock with the bones, half the wine, the water, onion, carrots and celery and simmer until the liquid is reduced by half. Put the hare meat into a basin together with the remaining wine and the rest of the ingredients and leave for 24 hours. Remove the hare, blot dry, brown in hot oil and transfer to a cast-iron, enamelled, casserole or thick saucepan. Strain the stock and add it, together with the marinade, to the meat. Cover, and bring to simmering point, and cook for 2 - 3 hours or until tender. The liquid should barely move. It may need longer if the hare is old, which it probably will be at the above weight. Add little bits of beurre manié (see p.167) until the sauce is of the required thickness, adjust the seasoning.

Serve with tagliatelle or spaghetti tossed in a little oil, and a salad of radiccio dressed with walnut oil and lemon juice.

Hare en Gelée with Thyme

This is a perfect dish for summer and a prime example of 'progressive cookery'. Supposing you have roasted a baron of hare, you will have the neck and forequarter left which you can freeze and then take out in the warmer weather for a cold supper or as part of a buffet. The recipe was given to me by Lucy's old nanny but she called it brawn, a name that I find puts people off, so I have adapted it and find it goes down a treat.

————————— Serves 2 - 4 —————————

1 neck and forequarter of hare
8 oz (250g) diced ham
1 shallot, peeled and chopped
1 tablespoon (15ml) redcurrant jelly
1 sprig each of thyme and parsley
1 strip lemon peel
1 glass sherry
stock (see p.160), or water and a stock cube
salt and pepper
1 tablespoon each chopped parsley and thyme
0.04 oz (11g) gelatine dissolved in a little
*   water (see p.163)*

Put everything except the chopped parsley and thyme into a casserole, cover with stock (see p.160) or water and a stock cube. Bring to the boil on top of the stove and simmer for 1½ – 2 hours, or until the meat falls off the bones. Pour into a colander sitting on top of a bowl and remove all the bones, the thyme, parsley and lemon peel. Reduce the liquid by fast boiling to 1 pint (600 ml), add the finely shredded meat, chopped thyme and parsley and gelatine. Stir well, and spoon into a 2 pint (1 litre) oiled mould. Leave to set and turn out.

Serve with baked potatoes or hot French bread and a salad of cubed beetroot in vinaigrette and sour cream sauce.

Dutch Hare Stew

This recipe was given to me by a keeper I met wildfowling in Holland with my Dutch host and artist Will Garfit. The stew he cooked in primitive conditions was delicious, and enabled us to get to sleep on hard bunks in an ancient hut on an island in the middle of a marsh during a Force 9 gale. The fruit blends well and the addition of white wine makes it less heavy.

———————— *Serves 6 - 8* ————————

1 hare cut into joints
flour for dredging
butter for frying
½ bottle white wine
½ pint (300 ml) stock (see p.160)
20 stoned prunes
4 oz (100g) chestnuts
1 pinch ground cloves
salt and pepper
potato or cornflour
1 tablespoon (15 ml) fromage frais (optional)

Dredge the hare joints with flour and brown in the butter. Place in a casserole with all the other ingredients and put into a pre-heated oven set at 400F/Gas Mark 6/200C. After 20 minutes turn down to 325F/Gas Mark 3/160C and leave for 2 -3 hours or until tender. If the sauce is too thin thicken with a little potato or cornflour mixed with cold water and stir in a tablespoonful fromage frais.

Serve with rice.

Hare Cakes

Any cold meat left over from roast hare can be made into a good supper dish, and a genuine 'progressive cookery' recipe.

——————— *Serves 2* ———————

8 oz (250g) left-over cooked hare meat
1 shallot, finely chopped
4 oz (125g) mashed potato
dried thyme
1 egg, beaten
1 dash Worcestershire Sauce
1 dash mushroom ketchup
salt and pepper
flour
beaten egg
breadcrumbs

Put the hare meat into the food processor and give a couple of sharp bursts, or mince it. Mix together with the potato, thyme, and seasonings. Make into balls, roll in flour, beaten egg and breadcrumbs and flatten into 6 cakes. Fry until golden.

Serve with fried bacon rolls, butter beans and a crisp green salad

Shaggy Inkcap Mushrooms

These mushrooms are also known by the delightful name of Lawyer's Wig. You may easily stumble on some of these when out in the country, but don't expect the hunter to bring them back with his prey as they are very fragile. You are in fact far more likely to find them on the edge of your lawn or by the compost heap. *Coprinus comatus* should be picked young, before the gills turn black. Its domed shape is quite easy to identify, with its fringed and shaggy appearance. The flesh should be white, and the gills white or pink and have a sweetish smell. They have passed their 'sell by date' by the time the gills turn black.

Fry in butter with fresh chopped parsley, chervil or tarragon.

NOTE: If you are interested in gathering wild fungi do invest in a good guide. There are several on the market. Courses on identification are often advertised in the papers and in gardening magazines, and it more than pays to go on one. The guide I use is *Mushrooms, and Other Fungi of Great Britain and Europe,* by Roger Phillips (Pan Books). This is a paperback tome; you need a pocket guide, too, for field work.

Sloe and Apple Jelly

A perfect excuse to gather some of the hedgerow harvest which is there for the taking. September or October are the best months to pick these fruits which you may easily spy growing in an ancient hedgerow or at the edge of a wood. Don't worry if the crab apples are out of reach, pick your sloes and freeze them, then mark your tree and go back after a gale has scattered the fruits. This makes a delicate, and slightly tart, jelly, just right to counteract the richness of a hare or venison stew.

Makes 3 x 1lb (500g) pots.

3 lbs (1.5kg) sloes
1 lb (500g) crab apples, neither peeled nor cored
sugar

Wash the fruit, place in pan with water to cover and cook until tender and mushy. Strain through a clean tea towel placed over a colander. Tie up and suspend over a basin to drip overnight. Transfer juice to a clean pan and add 1lb (500g) sugar to every pint (600ml) juice. Boil until set, skimming off any scum as it rises, then pour into heated pots and cover with cling film. Add lids or paper covers when cold.

Lemon Cream Brulée and Elderberry and Apple Jelly

This makes a light and slightly tart contrast to the richness of the hare. If possible serve in small white ramekins placed side by side on white plates (if you have them). The contrasting colours of the brulée and the deep purple of the jelly are very appetising. You can, of course, serve them as sweets in their own right if you so wish. Otherwise, use small glasses for the jelly and ramekins for the brulfle - this is vital as you have to place them under the grill, so containers must be heatproof. Bramble and apple or sloe and apple are equally good.

Serves 6

Lemon Cream Brulée

1 lemon
½ pint (300ml) double cream
1 tablespoon (15 ml) granulated or caster sugar
demerara sugar

Squeeze the lemon juice into a bowl. Bring the cream to the boil either in a saucepan or in the microwave for 3 minutes at full power (but watch it like a hawk) and then pour it in a steady stream from as high as possible onto the lemon juice. Stir in the sugar and spoon 2 tablespoons (30 ml) into each ramekin. Cool and place in coldest part of fridge to set. About 1 hour before serving sprinkle a good layer of demerara sugar over each ramekin and place under a very hot grill until the sugar has caramelized. If you have the grill hot enough it should only take a few seconds. Allow to cool and then serve with the jelly. If the hard topping melts, don't worry, it will still taste delicious.

Elderberry and Apple Jelly

1 lb (500g) each elderberries and crab apples or
cooking apples stewed and strained
sugar to taste
0.04oz (11g) gelatine
¾ pint (450ml) juice

Wash, but do not peel or core, the apples, stew them together with the elderberries in a little water until they are mushy, then strain. Make up the quantity with water if insufficient. Soak the gelatine in 1 tablespoon (15 ml) water and, when spongy, pour on the hot but not boiling, sweetened juice and stir until melted and pour into glasses or ramekins.

RABBIT

This amusing poaching story concerns my late husband Archie's shoot, which I still continue to run. The night before our first day, last season, the farmer from whom the ground is rented, rang up. His greeting was less than reassuring. "You've been poached," he said. "What the hell do you expect me to do about it?" I replied. "Don't worry. I've dealt with it," he said. It appears that on his way across the farm to milk the cows he had spied a beaten-up old Daihatsu, unlicensed and with no number plates, stuck in the middle of a field which, on closer investigation, was full of warm, freshly killed rabbits. He rushed back, got the JCB, lifted the Daihatsu up (having first removed the bunnies), transported it to another part of the farm and buried it! The next day two guys with lurchers appeared and asked, "You seen our car anywhere Guv?" "No," said my friend, and turning to his cowman he asked, "You seen a car about the place Bill?" "No," said Bill, "I ain't seen no cars nowhere." There the matter rests.

Another was told to me by a French friend who lives in the Sologne, the famous gameshooting area in France, and concerns a well-known local *braconnier* (poacher) called '*Le Lapin*' (the rabbit). He had been apprehended and was being walked along the canal by two policemen, one of whom had hold of his sleeve. All of a sudden he jerked free, dived into the water and swam to the other side, leaving the policeman holding the coat. As he reached the other bank he shouted, "You may have skinned '*le Lapin*' but you can't put him in the pot!"

Finally, a rabbit-poaching tale comes from an artist friend who, when he was at a well-known public school used to set snares in the surrounding woods. This was done on a Saturday so that he could visit them on a Sunday, when long gowns were worn which were ideal for concealing a bunny or two slung over the shoulders. All went well for some time until one Sunday when every wire had disappeared. At each site was a piece of paper bearing a different saying: 'the early bird catches the worm', ' if at first you don't succeed try, try, try again', 'he who laughs last laughs longest', 'better luck next time!' and so on. Once a week, post and parcels were doled out at breakfast time at each individual house table, and much anticipatory licking of lips took place as the parcels of goodies from home were opened. Some time later my friend received a large box which his pals opined would contain a cake. They were, however, disappointed and amazed for when it was undone all the missing rabbit wires fell out!

Rabbit is highly delicious but went out of favour with the advent of myxomatosis. There was always a slight stigma attached to it as being something only eaten by poorer people. In some cases it was probably the only meat seen in some cottages, the reason being its abundance. During the war it did sterling duty eking out the meat ration, and was served as chicken to the unsuspecting husbands of many of my mother's friends. Nowadays you have a choice of wild rabbit or the mass-produced farmed variety and it is widely available. The French are more discerning and the cookery supplements of any woman's magazine will as often as not include imaginative recipes for rabbit.

Beer and Rabbit Bourgeois

This country pâté was given to me by a friend who lived for a time in a small village near Beauvais. The recipe came from her *bonne à tout faire* and it has a good robust flavour. Better kept for a couple of days to let the flavours permeate.

———————————— *Serves 6 – 8* ————————————

1 lb (500g) uncooked rabbit meat taken off the
    bones and chopped finely
8 oz (250g) minced fat pork
¼ pint (150ml) light ale
1 teaspoon mixed herbs
2 bay leaves
salt and plenty of ground black pepper, or
    1 teaspoon crushed green peppercorns,
6 - 8 streaky bacon rashers, de-rinded

Marinate all the ingredients, except the bacon, overnight in the beer. Line a 1 pint (600ml) terrine with the rashers, reserving two. Fill with the marinade and meat mixture. Cover with the two remaining rashers and the bay leaves. Cook in a pre-heated oven at 350F/Gas Mark 4/175C for 1½ - 2 hours. Cool and refrigerate.

Roman Pie

When I was about ten years old my mother decided that I should have French lessons. The lady to whom I was sent included cookery in the curriculum. In fact, this was the only cooking I was ever taught. This was one of her recipes. It is very delicious, and you can substitute cooked pheasant or partridge for the rabbit.

―――――――――― *Serves 2 - 4* ――――――――――

butter
wholemeal breadcrumbs or crushed vermicelli
a double quantity shortcrust pastry (see p.164)
8 oz (250g) cooked macaroni
1 pint (600ml) cheese sauce, made with béchamel
*   sauce (see p.166) and 4 oz (125g) grated*
*   mature cheddar cheese*
meat from 1 cooked rabbit
2 chopped shallots
1 tablespoon (15ml) chopped parsley
salt and pepper

Butter a 7" (18cm) spring clip cake-tin and sprinkle with fresh breadcrumbs. Line with ⅔ of the pastry. Spoon the cooked macaroni into the dish, mix together the cheese sauce, chopped rabbit meat, shallots and parsley and pour it over the macaroni. Cover with the rest of the pastry, make a steam hole in the centre and cook in a pre-heated oven set at 400F/Gas Mark 6/200C for 1 hour.

Turn out onto a dish and serve with a salad of young spinach leaves, shredded sorrel, crisply fried garlic croûtons and crumbled bacon.

Rabbit and Chanterelles in Velouté Sauce

A delicious way of doing rabbit. I had it first in Brittany many years ago when I was staying with two elderly friends at their magical old chateau which seemed as though it had come straight out of 'Sleeping Beauty'. As far as I remember, I was recovering from what I fondly thought was a broken heart. My host believed that the best cure for this complaint was to eat a succession of gourmet dishes so he took me into the woods to look for ceps *(Boletus edulis)*, to accompany the rabbits which he had shot. Unfortunately, unless very skilled and lucky you are unlikely to find them over here, though two Italian restaurateur-friends of mine do so, but they have not divulged their secret locations so I use chanterelles *(Cantharellus cibarius)*. Failing these you can always fall back on dried ceps, porcini, or even field mushrooms *(Agaricus campestris)*.

———— Serves 2 - 4 ————

1 young rabbit, skinned and cut into joints
8 oz (250g) onion, peeled and chopped
1 garlic clove, peeled and chopped
4 oz (100g) butter
1 lb (500g) chanterelles or field mushrooms,
*   rinsed, drained and sliced*
or 2 (10g) packets porcini, soaked in a little hot
*   water*
6 rashers smoked streaky bacon, rolled and
*   secured with toothpicks*
1 good pinch dried thyme
salt and pepper
2 oz (50g) flour
¼ pint (150ml) dry cider
1 pint (600ml) stock (see p.160) or stock cube
*   and water*
2 tablespoons (30ml) crème fraîche

You can use farmed rabbit for this dish, but wild rabbit has a better flavour. Sauté the rabbit, onion and garlic in the butter and transfer to a casserole with the mushrooms, bacon rolls and seasonings. Sprinkle the flour into the pan and add the cider and stock, stirring well, then pour over the rabbit. Place in a pre-heated oven at 325F/Gas Mark 3/160C for 1½ – 2 hours or until tender. Transfer the rabbit pieces to a serving dish, reduce the sauce to ½ pint (300ml), stir in the créme fraîche and pour over.

Serve with pommes noisettes and buttered carrots

Savoury Rabbit with Tartare Sauce

Definitely a dinner party dish and one that does not need to masquerade as chicken.

─────────── *Serves 6 - 8* ───────────

2 young rabbits cut into suitable joints
1 tablespoon (15ml) oil
1 tablespoon (15ml) wine vinegar
1 small onion
1 slice of lemon
1 sprig each of parsley and thyme
salt and pepper
flour
1 egg, well beaten
fresh, fine breadcrumbs
oil for frying

Marinate the rabbit joints in the oil, vinegar, onion, lemon, herbs and seasoning for 3 hours. Remove joints from marinade and dry well. Roll in flour, dip in egg and coat with bread-crumbs. Deep fry at 325F (160C) for 5 - 10 minutes.

Serve with tartare sauce, potato purée and minted peas.

Rabbit Kebabs

A useful variation for a barbecue, but it can be grilled or cooked in the oven if rain stops play.

—————————— *Serves 2 - 4* ——————————

1 - 2 rabbits
8 – 10 rashers streaky bacon, de-rinded

Vinaigrette Salad Dressing

1 tablespoon (15ml) wine vinegar
4 tablespoons (60ml) olive oil
2 teaspoons mild Dijon mustard
2 teaspoons sugar
salt and pepper

Remove the meat from the rabbits, cut it into chunks and marinate in the salad dressing for 3 hours or more. When your barbecue is hot, roll each piece of rabbit in ½ a bacon rasher and stick on a skewer. Cook for 15 - 20 minutes, turning occasionally. To grill, place under a high heat, turning and basting once or twice until tender. If cooking in the oven pre-heat to 400F/Gas Mark 6/200C and cook for 30 minutes.

Serve with baked potatoes and a watercress salad.

Moroccan Rabbit with Raisins

I ate this high up in the Atlas Mountains in a fortress which had once belonged to the notorious Morrocan ruler *El Glaoui*. At the time when he was attending the coronation of Queen Elizabeth II, prisoners were manacled to the walls of the dungeons below the room in which we were eating. Our guide sensibly refrained from telling us this until we had finished our meal.

─────────── *Serves 6 - 8* ───────────

2 young rabbits cut into joints
4 oz (125g) butter
1 good pinch ground ginger and paprika
1 pinch ground nutmeg
3 crushed cardamon seeds
1 lb (500g) chopped onion
2 garlic cloves, peeled
1 pinch saffron
salt and ground black pepper
water
1 lb (500g) stoned raisins
1 tablespoon (15ml) honey
1 good pinch ground cinnamon
cornflour mixed with a little water
    (optional)
4 oz (125g) flaked almonds, fried
    until golden

Place the rabbit pieces in a casserole with everything except the honey, cinnamon, raisins and almonds. Cover with water and bring gently to the boil and then simmer for 1 hour. Add the raisins, and continue cooking for 30 minutes. Now add the honey and cinnamon. After 5 minutes remove from the stove, arrange the rabbit pieces on a dish, and cover with the raisins. If the sauce seems too thin, reduce it by fast boiling and thicken it with a little cornflour mixed with some water. Pour over the sauce and sprinkle with the almonds.

Serve with rice.

Harvest Rabbit Pie

I can remember the excitement when the reaper and binder got to the last few cuts in the field and the rabbits dashed out in all directions. Boys were there with sticks, and a farm worker or two with ancient hammer guns with damascus barrels, which certainly would not have passed the Birmingham Proof house. The resultant trophies were borne away with glee to be made into pie or pudding.

—————— *Serves 4 - 6* ——————

1 large rabbit cut into joints
8 oz (250g) bacon, diced
½ pint (300ml) stock (see p.160), or stock cube
*   and water*
1 tablespoon (15 ml) chopped parsley
1 teaspoon grated lemon rind
salt and pepper
3 hard boiled eggs
1 lb (500g) puff pastry
1 egg, beaten

Simmer the rabbit and other ingredients, except the eggs, for 1½ hours, adding more stock if necessary. Leave to get cold, then transfer to a 3 pint (1.8 litre) pie dish, reserving half the stock. Lay the hard boiled eggs, cut into quarters, over the top and cover with puff pastry (I use bought). Make a hole in the centre and glaze with the beaten egg. Bake in a pre-heated oven set at 425F/Gas Mark 7/220C for 30 - 35 minutes or until golden.

Serve with new potatoes, and broad beans tossed in butter and sprinkled with chopped, fresh marjoram.

Tartare Sauce

If you want to return to basics you could make your tartare sauce with home-pickled nasturtium seeds instead of capers. Nearly all cottage gardens used to have a glorious clash of colour, most of which came from the brilliant scarlets, oranges and yellows of the nasturtiums, the leaves of which are delicious added to a salad, giving it a slightly peppery flavour.

————————— *Serves 4 - 6* —————————

basic mayonnaise (see p.168)
1 shallot or small onion, peeled and very finely
*   chopped*
1 or 2 finely chopped gherkins
1 teaspoon finely chopped capers
2 teaspoons finely chopped parsley, tarragon or
*   sorrel*

Make a basic mayonnaise (see p.168) and stir in the chopped shallot or onion, the chopped gherkins, capers and herbs.

Pickled Nasturtium Seeds

Be sure to pick your nasturtium seeds on a dry day.

nasturtium seeds
1 pint (600ml) distilled malt vinegar
2 bay leaves
2 teaspoons salt
6 peppercorns

Dry your seeds on a tray in the sun or in a very slow oven set at 250F/Gas Mark½/120C. Bring the rest of the ingredients to the boil, then allow to get completely cold. Pack the dried seeds into a sterilised jar and cover with the vinegar. Seal and keep for 2 months before use.

Damson Cobbler

A really traditional country pudding with a scone topping. Make a double quantity of the mixture and bake some scones with what's left over from the pudding.

—————————— *Serves 4 - 6* ——————————

1½ lbs (750g) damsons
sugar to sweeten
cobbler topping, made with 4 oz (125g) flour (see p.165)

Cook the fruit in a pan with 1 tablespoon water and some sugar until the juice begins to run and the fruit is cooked. Adjust sweetening and spoon into a 2 pint (1 litre) shallow, fireproof dish. Roll out the cobbler topping to ½" (1cm) thick, then cut into 2" (5cm) rounds. Lay these in overlapping rows on the fruit and bake in a pre-heated oven set at 425F/Gas Mark 7/220C for 20 minutes.

VENISON

After leaving the army, Archie did a year's stint as professional stalker on a friend's estate in Scotland. As meat was still rationed there was a great incentive for people to poach deer as the venison fetched a tidy sum on the black market. At one time this estate was plagued by a particular gang of poachers, who they could never catch, but one day Nemesis, in the person of Archie, caught up with them. During the course of a stalk he spied their white van parked up a little-used track, so he went to investigate and realized that they were about their nefarious business. A lighted match in the petrol tank did the trick, and they never appeared again. A bonus was the cache of several dead beasts which were discovered by Archie and his friend.

Venison is roughly divided into three categories: red deer, fallow and roe. Red deer should be hung for at least a week in a cool, fly-proof place to tenderise, before steeping in a marinade for 24 hours, or longer. Larding, or barding with pork fat, is essential as it is a very lean meat and can be very dry. Fallow often has quite a covering of fat and if it is a young beast will not really need marinating. Roe is, to my mind, the gourmet of the three, and though lean, will not need any extra attention other than frequent basting. Venison is becoming popular because of its healthy image and is available in most supermarkets at the appropriate season. This is generally farmed red deer which does not have such a 'gamey' taste.

Venison Terrine with Pink Peppercorns

This meltingly delicious terrine makes an excellent cold buffet dish for the summer and, with hunks of fresh bread and farm butter could be the centre piece of a picnic.

——————— Serves 6 – 8 ———————

12 oz (350g) venison, (neck or shoulder), diced
6 oz (175g) roe liver or calves liver
8 oz (250g) fat belly of pork, diced
6 - 8 smoked streaky bacon rashers
1 thick slice of bread with crusts cut off
2 eggs, well beaten
2 tablespoons (30 ml) port
4 oz (100g) onion, peeled and finely chopped
½ teaspoon grated orange rind
1 teaspoon pink peppercorns (obtainable in
  supermarkets or delicatessen in jars of brine)
1 or 2 sprigs of thyme or a couple of bay leaves
salt and ground black pepper

Chop the venison, liver and half the pork roughly, either by hand or in a food processor or pass once through a mincer. Transfer to a mixing bowl. Then process the rest of the pork until it is really smooth or pass it twice though a mincer. Soak the bread in the beaten egg and port and add to the mixture with the rest of the ingredients except the rashers, and mix well. Cut the rinds off the rashers and stretch with the back of a knife. Lay the branches of thyme or bayleaves on the bottom of a 2 lb (1 kg) loaf tin or 2 pint (1 litre) terrine with the bacon rashers and fill with the mixture. Lay some more rashers over the top and cover with foil. (If you are using a terrine put the thyme on top of the final layer of rashers as you won't be turning it out). Stand in a roasting pan and pour boiling water to come half way up the side of the tin or terrine. Place in a pre-heated oven at 350F/Gas Mark 4/180C for 1½ hours or until the juice runs clear when pierced with a skewer. When nearly cool place a weight on top and leave until quite cold. Refrigerate for a minimum of two days for the flavours to develop. To serve, turn out and slice.

A salad of celeriac and apple cut into julienne strips, lightly blanched and then mixed with half mayonnaise and half fromage frais makes a good accompaniment.

Anthony's Way with Roe Haunch

Anthony is a young friend who is a very skilled stalker. He told me this rather charming poaching story. An elderly friend who lived in Scotland had just had a hip operation. Nonetheless, as soon as he got home he decided to celebrate being out of hospital. So he got out his Land Rover, drove to the moor and let his lurchers out for a run. Unfortunately, a roebuck got up and they chased it into a wood on his neighbour's land where they killed it. Determined not to be beaten by his disability he drove up and with the greatest difficulty, for he was on crutches, managed to manhandle it into the back of the vehicle. The following week he went to dinner with his neighbour. When they got to the port his host said, "A most extraordinary thing happened last week. I saw somebody with a Land Rover apparently having great trouble, as he was on crutches, heaving a roebuck into the back. I wonder who it could have been?" Anthony's friend, like the Tar Baby with Brer Rabbit, said nothing; his crutches were leaning by his chair and the matter was never referred to again.

This is Anthony's way of cooking a haunch of roe deer.

——————————— *Serves 6 - 8* ———————————

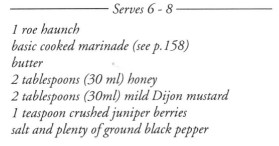

1 roe haunch
basic cooked marinade (see p.158)
butter
2 tablespoons (30 ml) honey
2 tablespoons (30ml) mild Dijon mustard
1 teaspoon crushed juniper berries
salt and plenty of ground black pepper

Marinate the haunch for 2 - 3 days then remove and dry well. Pre-heat oven to 450F/Gas Mark 8/230C and melt the butter in a roasting pan until foaming. Cover the haunch with a paste of honey, mustard and juniper berries, sprinkle with salt and pepper and put in the pan with ½ pint (300ml) of the marinade. Baste, and put in the oven for a good hot blast for 20 minutes, then baste again. Cover with a tent of foil and reduce the heat to 375F/Gas Mark 5/190C for 20 minutes to the lb (500kg) basting frequently. Reduce the strained marinade to ¼ pint (150ml). When the haunch is cooked transfer to a serving dish, add the marinade to the pan juices, re-heat and pour into a sauce boat.

A purée of swede, flavoured with grated nutmeg, and a sliced gratin of potatoes goes well. The latter can be cooked in the oven at the same time as the haunch. Slice some potatoes on the fine blade of your food processor and place in a shallow dish in layers, with bits of butter, cover with boiling milk and season well with salt and pepper. Sprinkle the top with fresh breadcrumbs and Parmesan cheese.

NOTE: If you have a clay brick or Romertoft, place your haunch in the clay pot, cover with the honey and mustard mixture, put on the lid and place in a cold oven. Switch to 475F/Gas Mark 9/ 240C and leave for 2 hours. Turn the joint over after 1 hour.

Carole's Roe with Port and Cream

Carole and her parents live in the Sologne where they shoot and eat a lot of game. This is actually her recipe for cooking leg of wild boar, but haunch of roe is equally good done this way.

———————— *Serves 6 - 8* ————————

1 roe haunch
basic cooked marinade (see p.158)
salt and pepper
1 oz (25g) butter
1 oz (25g) flour
½ glass port
crème fraîche

Marinate the haunch for 3 days, turning it from time to time. Transfer it to a roasting pan with the vegetables from the marinade and some of the liquid. Season, and place in a pre-heated oven set at 425F/Gas Mark 7/220C for 15 – 20 minutes to the lb (500g), depending on how rare you like it. While it is roasting make a roux with the butter and flour, the rest of the marinade and the port and let it simmer for half an hour. When the meat is cooked, place it on a serving dish. Pour the sauce into the roasting pan. Stir and scrape well, add some crème fraîche and strain into a jug.

Garnish with baked apples filled with red currant jelly. Alternatively, surround with mounds of apple and chestnut purée or scatter cranberries round the joint. Serve with a purée of celeriac and potato.

Boned Saddle of Roe en Croûte

This is for the occasion when you want to impress and astonish your guests. It is quite easy to bone a saddle yourself, but if you feel faint-hearted get your friendly butcher to do it for you (if you still have one in your part of the world!).

———————— *Serves 6 - 8* ————————

4 oz (125g) butter
2 lbs (1 kg) boned roe saddle
¼ pint (150ml) red wine
2 shallots, peeled and finely chopped
8 oz (250g) mushrooms, chopped
shortcrust pastry (see p.164)
1 tablespoon rowan jelly
1 teaspoon dried thyme
¼ pint (150ml stock), or stock cube and water
salt and ground black pepper

Pre-heat oven to 425F/Gas Mark 7/220C and heat butter until foaming. Put in the saddle and baste well. Cook for 15 minutes then remove and allow to get quite cold. Swill pan out with red wine and pour into a small saucepan. Sautée the shallots and mushrooms in the remainder of the butter and cool. Roll out three quarters of the pastry and lay it in the bottom of a clean roasting pan. Place the saddle on top, season with salt and pepper, spread with the jelly, three quarters of the shallots and mushrooms and sprinkle on the thyme. Brush inside each corner with water. Bring the pastry up the sides of the meat and pinch each corner together. Brush the edges with water. Roll out the remaining pastry, brush round the edge with water and lay over the top, sealing the edges so that the whole thing is encased. Make one or two slits in the top, decorate with pastry leaves and brush with the beaten egg. Place in a pre-heated oven set at 425F/Gas Mark 7/220C for 15 minutes, then turn down to 375F/Gas Mark 5/190C for 20 minutes. Allow to rest for 15 minutes before carving.

While it is resting, make the sauce. To the wine in the saucepan add the remainder of the shallots, mushrooms and the stock. Adjust seasoning and reduce to half by fast boiling. If it tastes tart add a little jelly.

As it is very rich, serve with new potatoes and dandelion and rocket salad dressed with walnut oil and lemon juice.

It more than pays to transplant some errant dandelions into your kitchen garden and nurture them. Before they flower cover them with a flower pot and blanch them. In France they are cultivated and you can buy packets of seed. The French have two names - *dent de lion* (lion's teeth) and *pisse-en-lit* (wet your bed), aptly referring to its diuretic properties!

Forester's Goulash with Dumplings

Baron Karl Anton Von Langen came into our lives many years ago. He was a dedicated hunter and never got over the fact that his estate in Eastern Germany had been annexed by the communists so he used to come pigeon shooting with Archie. At 79 he thought nothing of getting up at dawn to go roe stalking, then a day's pigeon shooting which was rounded off by an evening stalk. He had a huge fund of recipes for venison and this is one of them.

———————— *Serves 6 - 8* ————————

3 oz (75g) fat bacon, cut into small dice
2 oz (50g) lard or bacon dripping
3 onions, peeled and chopped
2 lb (1 kg) venison, cut into 1" (3 cm) cubes
4 oz (100g) cooked gammon
bay leaves
1 teaspoon dried thyme
2 tablespoons chopped parsley
3 - 4 juniper berries
3 peppercorns
1 teaspoon mild paprika
salt and pepper
1½ pints (850ml) stock (see p.160) or water
  and a stock cube
1 oz (25g) flour
½ pint (275ml) sour cream or smetana

Fry the cubes of bacon in the lard or dripping until transparent, add the onions and cook until golden, then brown the venison add the herbs, seasoning and stock and simmer, covered, on top of the stove until tender, about 1½ - 2 hours. Mix the flour with the cream and add to the stew together with the gammon.

This is a real peasant dish so serve with breadcrumb dumplings, boiled potatoes and sauerkraut or white cabbage with caraway seeds.

Stalker's Pie

A severe case of 'progressive cookery'. Roast venison is rich and the meat is dense and filling so there is usually quite a lot left over which I make into a variation of Cottage Pie.

————————— *Serves 4 - 6* —————————

1 onion, peeled and chopped
2 oz (50g) butter
2 oz (50g) flour
¾ pint (450ml) stock made from the bones of the
haunch (see p.160)
1 glass red wine
1 lb (500g) approximately, cooked venison,
minced or chopped in the food processor
8 oz (250g) cooked or tinned chestnuts, roughly
chopped
4 oz (125g) button mushrooms
1 tablespoon (15ml) concentrated tomato purée
1 teaspoon rowan jelly
1 teaspoon mixed herbs
salt and black pepper
mashed potato made from 1½ lbs (800g) boiled
potatoes

Fry the onion in the butter then add the flour and cook for a few seconds, pour in the stock and red wine and cook until thick. Tip in all the other ingredients and mix well. Pour into a 2 pint (1 litre) pie dish and cover with mashed potato. Cook in the oven set at 425F/Gas Mark 7/220C for 20 - 30 minutes. If preferred, the mixture can be cooled and then covered with puff pastry and cooked in a pre-heated oven set at 425F/Gas Mark 7/220C for 30 – 40 minutes.

Serve with leeks in a cheese sauce au gratin. They can be cooked in the oven with the pie.

Stalker's Breakfast

If your personal stalker should happen on a Giant Puffball, *Langermannia Gigantea,* while flitting through the grassy glades, threaten him with dire penalties if he doesn't pick it. With the liver of a freshly killed beast it makes an unforgettable breakfast.

—— *Serves 4 (or 2 very hungry stalkers)* ——

butter or bacon fat for frying
4 rashers of bacon
4 slices of bread
4 slices 1"(2cm) thick Giant Puffball coated in egg
*   and breadcrumb*
fresh roe liver and kidneys
4 eggs

Heat the fat and fry the bacon and bread, then the puff ball slices until golden. Add some more fat and cook the kidneys, and the liver which you have sliced very thinly, for a few seconds on each side. It should still be pink. Finally fry the eggs.

Serve with potato scones, farmhouse butter, homemade marmalade and tea.

Breadcrumb Dumplings

These dumplings are excellent served with any stew and would have been approved of by my daughter Lucy's nanny, as a thrifty way of using up stale bread. Real 'progressive cookery', as any left over dumplings can be fried in egg and breadcrumbs and served with roast or cold game.

Makes approximately 24 dumplings.

2 oz (50g) butter or margarine
8 oz (250g) breadcrumbs
2 tablespoons (30ml) chopped parsley
2 eggs
1 tablespoon (15ml) flour
salt

Cream the fat until soft, add the eggs, breadcrumbs, flour and parsley and salt and mix well. Leave to stand for 30 minutes. Make teaspoonfuls into tiny balls and poach gently for 3 – 4 minutes in boiling water.

Steamed Honey Pudding

When I was a child beehives were a common sight in villages and in some very rural areas I remember the bees were kept in straw bee skeps (an old fashioned hive). We had an old jobbing gardener called Mr Funge who was reputed to be a woman hater, but children obviously didn't count for I was occasionally invited into his thatched cottage for a glass of homemade ginger beer. The garden was exactly as we all imagine, full of hollyhocks, mignonette and a beautiful vegetable garden. When I left he always gave me a pot of his honey. The only time he ever left the village was on one occasion when he went to London by train to collect a particularly special Italian queen bee. This species has the reputation of being very fierce, and to my father's consternation Mr Funge proceeded to show everyone in the railway carriage the queen bee, which he produced from his waistcoat pocket in a matchbox.

———————— *Serves 4 - 6* ————————

1 oz (25g) ground rice
1 pint (600ml) milk
6 oz (175g) fresh white breadcrumbs
4 oz (100g) honey
1 pinch ground ginger
rind of ½ lemon, finely grated
2 egg yolks
1 oz (25g) butter
2 egg whites

Cook the ground rice in the milk for 10 minutes and stir into the breadcrumbs, honey, ginger and grated lemon rind. Add the egg yolks and beat well for some minutes. Finally, whisk the egg whites till they are stiff and fold gently into the mixture. Spoon into a buttered 1½ pint (900ml) pudding basin, cover with buttered foil and steam for 2 hours.

Serve with a sauce made with honey, lemon juice and apple purée.

Ginger Beer

This is really refreshing and goes down very well at a picnic or in the packed lunch of a stalker (or poacher).

Makes approximately 6 x 1 pint (600ml) bottles.

8 oz (250g) sugar
1 gallon (3.5 litres) water
1 level tablespoon (15ml) dried yeast
1 level teaspoon ground ginger
juice of 1 lemon
extra sugar for bottling
Campden tablets for sterilizing equipment

Thoroughly wash and sterilize a plastic container using the Campden tablets. Dissolve the sugar in a little of the water, but do not allow to boil. Cool until tepid and add the yeast, ginger and lemon juice. Pour the remainder of the water into the container and stir well. Cover and stand in a warm place for a week. Sterilize 6 - 8 x 1 pint (600ml) screw top bottles with Campden tablets. Pour in the ginger beer, adding ½ teaspoon sugar to each 1 pint (600ml) bottle and screw tops on tightly. Drink after a week. When pouring, be careful not to disturb any sediment which may have settled at the bottom of the bottle.

WILD BOAR

Wild boar has not been hunted in Britain for centuries, but on the continent and in Russia and Eastern Europe it is a much prized quarry. My only brush with a wild boar occurred during a visit to Austria in the early 1960s. Archie and I were invited to accompany an aged scion of the Austrian nobility on a commercial boar shoot. Being penurious as a result of the war, he had married an American heiress and he was dependant on her to subsidise his sport. As we waited in the forest for the beaters to approach we suddenly saw a huge boar with enormous tusks advancing towards us. It came closer and closer and was soon well within range but the old man made no move to shoot. Archie said afterward that he was getting worried for my safety and was preparing to seize the rifle and administer the *coup de grâce*, but luckily the beast turned and trotted off. We came to the conclusion that the old Prince had done his sums and decided that his wife was unlikely to stump up the $2000 or so which this magnificent trophy would have cost him had he shot it! I have heard that since the Iron Curtain came down between Hungary and Austria many wild boar from Hungary have been taking advantage of their new found freedom and have been crossing the border into the Austrian forests where their numbers have to be controlled.

Boar is now being farmed in this country and is available from some supermarkets and from some mail order suppliers. The taste is not as strong as the truly wild variety and any you buy is likely to be young so the length of time you leave it in the marinade can be shortened. The flavour is much like pork but with a slightly 'gamey' taste.

Inige's Wild Boar Chops

On the trail of a good recipe for wild boar, I rang a Dutch friend of mine on his car phone. After a few seconds' conversation he said, "Could you hold on for a moment?" so I naturally imagined he had a client to whom he was talking. I heard a muffled thump and he came back on the phone and said, "That's another pigeon shot!" Far from being an important meeting, it transpired that he was in a hide shooting pigeons which were damaging a field of corn! The following is his sister Inige's recipe for boar chops. She tells me that boar mince makes particularly delicious cottage pie, lasagne or moussaka.

—————— *Serves 2* ——————

4 boar chops

Marinade

½ bottle rosé wine
2 tablespoons (30 ml) olive oil
1 leek, 1 piece celery, 1 carrot, 1 clove garlic,
*   chopped*
6 juniper berries, crushed
2 bay leaves
1 tablespoon parsley, chopped
pepper

4 oz (125g) butter
4 oz (125g) onion
2 oz (50g) bacon, diced
3 oz (75g) flour
salt and pepper

Lay the chops in a shallow china dish and pour over the marinade ingredients and leave in a cool place or at the bottom of the fridge for up to two days. If using farmed boar, it will not need so long. Remove the chops and set aside. Melt the butter and fry the onion and bacon. Add the flour and cook until golden, then pour in the marinade (with vegetables), stirring constantly until the sauce thickens. Season, then simmer on a very low heat for

1 hour. Dry the chops well with kitchen paper, then fry in butter for 10 minutes on each side. Strain the sauce over them and simmer for a further 5 minutes.

Serve with braised chicory and boiled potatoes.

Czechoslavakian Wild Boar

A friend told me the following tale which may be apocryphal, but it is so bizarre that no one could have made it up. A man went boar shooting in Czechoslavakia. The accomodation was in a rather primitive hut in the middle of the forest. There were no 'mod cons' and a utensil was provided under the bed for use at night. On the last day the *Jagd Meister* (shoot organiser) told the shooting party that there would be a special dinner that evening with wild boar stew as the main course. After the soup the guests waited with much anticipatory licking of lips for the advent of the boar stew. To their consternation, when it finally arrived, it was borne in by the head keeper in one of the chamber pots!

This recipe comes from *The Bohemian Kitchen 1877* and was translated from the Czeck by the friend who gave it to me.

———————— *Serves 2 - 4* ————————

2 lbs (1kg) boned leg of wild boar

Marinade

½ pint (300ml) water
¼ pint (150ml) wine vinegar
4oz carrot, celery and parsley, chopped
5 peppercorns
5 juniper berrries
5 chilli seeds
3 bay leaves
1 pinch dried thyme

salt
1 tablespoon (15ml) German mustard
1 teaspoon dried thyme
1 pinch crushed chillies
ground black pepper
1 piece lemon peel
2-3 tomatoes, sliced
¼ pint (150ml) white wine
4oz (125g) pork dripping, lard or butter
2 large onions, peeled and thickly sliced

Place the boar meat in a china bowl and cover with the marinade ingredients. Leave in a cool place or at the bottom of the fridge for 3 days, turning from time to time. Remove and dry well, rub with salt and cover with mustard, thyme, chillies, pepper, lemon peel and sliced tomatoes. Place in a roasting pan with the dripping and roast in a pre-heated oven set at 375F/Gas Mark 5/ 190C for 1½ hours. Baste frequently and after 30 minutes pour the white wine over the meat. Slice onto a warm serving dish and pour over the strained juices from the roasting tin.

Serve with roast potatoes and cranberry compôte.

Baked Jam Roly Poly

Suet puddings were staple diet in the country and could be spread with left-over, minced, cold meat or used to make a small quantity of fresh, cooked mince go further. As a puddding it filled in any hungry corners after a meagre first course. This can be steamed or boiled but baking is easier as you don't have a nasty, soggy, tea towel to cope with afterwards.

——————— *Serves 6 - 8* ———————

8 oz (300g) self raising flour
1 pinch salt
3 oz (75g) shredded suet
cold water to mix
1 lb (500g) jam

Sift flour and salt into a bowl and add the suet and enough water to make a soft dough. Roll out into an oblong about ½" (1cm) thick and spread generously with jam, leaving a border round the edge. Wet this with water and roll the pastry into a bolster. Place in a greased baking tin and bake in a pre-heated oven set at 400F/Gas Mark 6/200C for 45 minutes to 1 hour.

Serve with a sauce made by heating jam and lemon juice.

SQUIRREL

Not liking to write about things which I have not tried myself, I prevailed upon a friend's gardener to get me two squirrels. Having skinned and 'paunched' them (they are extremely tough to skin) I decided to cook them and have a 'tasting'. None of my friends, and that includes country folk, would even entertain the idea, shaking their heads and saying, "Ugh! how could you?" The only person who was game was Mike, a dear friend who lives in the East End of London.

The flavour of squirrel is rich and succulent, which is not surprising since it lives on nuts and berries and, of course, in the spring the eggs of song and game birds, which is why the Grey Squirrel *(Sciurus carolinensis)* is so abhorred by gamekeepers.

Fricassée of Squirrel

In many North American cookery books squirrel features in recipes for Brunswick Pie, but I decided to cook it in a way that would give the meat the best chance to retain its special flavour. Initially, I had thought of cooking the squirrels in a cream sauce, but on tasting the stewed squirrel I decided that it was so rich it would be better suited to a fricassée. And so it proved. It was so scrummy that we both had second helpings and agreed that it could easily grace any gourmet dinner party.

serves 2 - 4

2 squirrels, skinned, paunched and jointed
1 onion stuck with 2 cloves
1 carrot
1 bay leaf
salt and pepper
2 oz (50g) butter
2 oz (50g) flour
1 pint (600ml) game or chicken stock (see p.160)
    or water and a chicken stock cube
fromage frais (optional)

Stew the squirrels in the stock with the onion, carrot, bay leaf and seasoning until very tender. This will take about 1½ hours. Make a béchamel sauce with the butter, flour and stock, and add the squirrel meat which you have taken off the bones. Stir in a little fromage frais to counteract the richness.

Serve with basmati rice and a frisée salad dressed with lemon juice and hazelnut oil.

NOTE: To 'paunch' is to remove the 'innards'.

Fried Squirrel with Toasted Hazelnuts

You can only do this with young squirrels. How do you tell which is a young squirrel? You may well ask, but I go by the theory that small ones are probably young. One of the two that I used in the previous recipe must definitely have been the grand-father of all squirrels as he was twice as big as the other one and tougher to skin.

—————————— *Serves 2 - 4* ——————————

2 squirrels, skinned, paunched and jointed
flour to coat
butter for frying
lemon juice
1 dash soy sauce
2 tablespoons (30ml) single cream
1 tablespoon (15ml) toasted, chopped hazelnuts

Coat the squirrels in the flour and fry gently in the butter until tender, then remove to a serving dish, and keep hot. Add a few drops of lemon juice and the soy sauce to the pan juices and finally the cream. Let it all bubble for a few seconds, pour it over the squirrel joints and then sprinkle on the hazelnuts.

Serve with new potatoes and a spinach and sorrel purée.

Steamed Nut Pudding with Redcurrant Sauce

If you are lucky you may be able to beat the squirrels to it and pick some hazelnuts for this unusual steamed pudding. The recipe was given to me by an Austrian friend who used to come pigeon shooting with Archie. If redcurrants are unavailable, use raspberries, strawberries or anything that takes your fancy to make the sauce.

——————— *Serves 4 - 6* ———————

2 oz (50g) butter
2 oz (50g) sugar
3 egg yolks
3 egg whites
1 oz (25g) white breadcrumbs
1 oz (25g) plain flour
2 oz (25g) toasted, chopped hazelnuts
fruit of your choice
icing sugar

Put the butter, half the sugar and the egg yolks into the food processor and cream well then tip into a mixing bowl. Whisk the egg whites until stiff and add the remaining sugar and whip again until stiff. Fold into the creamed mixture with the crumbs, flour and nuts. Spoon into a buttered and floured 1½ pint (900ml) pudding basin, cover with foil and steam for 1 hour. To make the sauce, put the chosen fruit with half its weight of icing sugar into the food processor and blend well, then press through a sieve. If you decide to use blackberries or blackcurrants they will need to be gently cooked over a low heat with little or no water, to extract the juice and bring out the flavour.

SALMON

It is a far cry from the days when it was written into a domestic servant's contract that salmon was not to be served more than twice a week. Sadly, the wild salmon stocks are dwindling and the chances of any poacher being much the richer after a night's work are pretty slim. A niece of Archie's remembers going down to their local river in Argyllshire when she was a child before the war, and he showed her how to 'guddle'. This resulted in a 7½ lb salmon which they had to pretend had been caught by legal methods, as Archie's brother would have been exceedingly displeased if he had known the real means of it's capture.

A friend told me a story of a man who used to take a beat on a well-known English salmon river. If there was nothing doing on his bit of water he used to think nothing of fishing other people's beats. Owners and rods were wary of remonstrating with him as he had, in the past, been a friend of a certain pair of well-known criminals and his companions appeared to have menacing bulges under their coats!

Smoked Salmon and Fried Almond Pâté

This is a light pâté with a crunchy texture. It is easy and quick to make and freezes well.

———————— Serves 6 - 8 ————————

8 oz (250g) smoked salmon
juice of ½ lemon, or more if required
2 oz (50g) butter
2 teaspoons Hellman's mayonnaise
1 teaspoon horseradish sauce
3 tablespoons (45ml) crème fraîche
1 pinch cayenne pepper
1 teaspoon dried dill
1 oz (25g) flaked almonds
lemon slice and melted butter for decoration

Chop the smoked salmon up roughly and put in the food processor with the lemon juice. Switch on and whizz until smooth. Fry the almonds in the butter until golden then drain the butter into a jug and transfer the almonds to a plate. With the motor running pour the butter through the funnel and then the rest of the ingredients. Reserve a few almonds for decoration and tip the remainder into the processor. Whizz for a second or two until mixed in but not finely chopped. Spoon into a 1 pint (600ml) dish or terrine and refrigerate.

When quite cold, decorate with the reserved almonds and a slice of lemon and pour over a thin layer of melted butter.

Barbecued Whole Salmon

A fresh run fish, newly caught, cut into steaks and fried in butter is as near to culinary heaven as you are likely to get, but if you want to cook a whole salmon the following produces good results. Try wrapping your fish – the one I experimented with weighed 10lbs (4.5 - 5kg) in an issue of *The Daily Telegraph*, *The Times* or similar (not tabloids!) completely soaked and sodden.

Place on a barbecue, cook until both sides are charred, then peel off the paper and skin carefully.

Place a lump of sorrel butter on each plate and serve with watercress salad and baked potatoes.

Poached Whole Salmon

No pun intended! Rather like making Hollandaise sauce, cooking a whole salmon seems to induce feelings of panic in the putative cook. Provided you own, or can borrow, a fish kettle it is really very easy and the end result lends itself to a host of ideas for 'progressive cookery'.

> *1 salmon*
> *water, to which has been added 1 tablespoon*
> *(15ml) salt and 1 tablespoon (15ml) vinegar*
> *to each quart (1 litre), or court bouillon (see p.161)*

Place the fish in the cold liquid and bring slowly to simmering point. Turn off the heat, put on the lid and leave until cold. Remove fish, cover with a cucumber and lemon aspic and serve with sorrel mayonnaise.

If it is to be eaten hot, bring the court bouillon to simmering point and then poach the salmon for 4 minutes to the lb (500g). Remove and serve with plain boiled potatoes and Hollandaise sauce.

Salmon Baked in Foil

This obviates the necessity for a fish kettle and a lot of people prefer to cook their salmon this way. Lay your fish on a well buttered sheet of foil on a roasting pan. Oil the foil if the salmon is to be eaten cold. Fill the stomach cavity of the fish with sprigs of fennel or dill, slices of lemon, pepper and salt. Seal the foil and make into a loose parcel. If it is too tight the steam won't be able to circulate. Pre-heat the oven to 375F/Gas Mark5/190C and cook for 8 minutes to the 1lb (500g).

If the salmon is to be eaten hot, leave it to stand for 10 minutes before unwrapping. To eat it cold, leave it in the foil parcel until cool and then refrigerate.

Salmon Kedegree

I make no apologies for including this delicious excuse for 'progressive cookery'. It seems hard to realise that this was, during the 'Season', always part of the array of dishes to be found on the sideboard for breakfast. I can remember, even before the last war, what my godmother's house guests could expect to see when they entered the dining room. Sausages, bacon, scrambled eggs, cold ham, cold grouse, woodcock or partridge and kedgeree, trout or herrings in oatmeal or kippers! For my part it is one of my 'top ten' supper dishes.

─────── *Serves 4 - 6* ───────

1 tablespoon (15ml) sunflower oil
12 oz (350g) basmati rice
4 oz (125g) butter
¼ pint (150ml) single cream or crème fraîche
1 tablespoon (15ml) finely minced onion
1 tablespoon (15ml) parsley, finely chopped
1 pinch curry powder
1 squeeze lemon juice
salt and plenty of freshly ground black pepper
8 - 12 oz (250 - 350g) cooked salmon
4 hard boiled eggs, roughly chopped

Heat the oil in a saucepan then tip in the rice, shake well to coat, and then pour in boiling water to 1" (2cm) above the level of the rice. Cover and cook over a low heat for 15 minutes. Turn off heat, place a folded tea towel over the top of the saucepan and replace the lid and leave for a further 15 – 20 minutes. Now stir in the rest of the ingredients and heat through, adding even more cream or butter if it seems dry.

A green salad is the best accompaniment, and some marrow chutney.

Salmon Croquettes

This is an excellent way to make use of left-over cooked fish, for if you do not want to eat the croquettes straight away they can be frozen individually on a baking sheet and then transferred to a freezer bag. You can then cook 1 or 2 for supper, or if someone turns up unexpectedly, you have the perfect 'convenience' meal to hand.

Makes approximately 12 croquettes.

————————— *Serves 4 - 6* —————————

8 oz (250g) cooked salmon
¼ pint (150ml) béchamel sauce (see p.166)
1 teaspoon onion, finely chopped
1 teaspoon lemon juice
1 tablespoon (15ml) chopped dill or fennel
1 hard-boiled egg, finely chopped
1 pinch cayenne
salt and pepper
flour to dredge
1 egg, well beaten, to coat
breadcrumbs (undyed if possible) to coat
sunflower oil for frying

Mix the salmon, béchamel sauce, onion, lemon juice, herbs, hard boiled egg and seasoning. When cool, take a dessert-spoonful and roll it into a cork shape. Repeat until all the mixture has been used. Dredge with flour, dip in the beaten egg and coat in the breadcrumbs. Fry in deep fat until golden and drain on kitchen paper.

Serve with pommes frîtes and braised fennel.

Salmon Tart with Chanterelles

If you are lucky enough to catch your fish in a Scottish river and there are some birch woods nearby the chances are that you may find some chanterelles, *Cantharellus cibarius,* those lovely orange fungi that look like parasols blown inside out. They make a delicious combination in a tart but if neither of these options is open to you, just buy some fresh salmon and team it with either shitake, oyster, chestnut or ordinary button mushrooms.

──────── *Serves 6 - 8* ────────

4 oz (125g) onion, peeled and chopped
2 oz (50g) butter
5 oz (125g) chanterelles
1 lb (500g) salmon
1 ¼ pint béchamel sauce
1 pinch grated nutmeg
salt and pepper
4 hard-boiled eggs, sliced in rings
3 oz (75g) créme fraîche
shortcrust pastry, made with 12 oz (350g)
flour (see p.164)

Sweat the onions in the butter, then add the chanterelles. Poach the salmon gently in a little water and lemon juice for 5 minutes. Make a béchamel sauce (see p.166) with the flour, butter and milk and add the seasonings, onion and the chanterelles. Meanwhile make the pastry and line a 10" (25cm) flan dish with the pastry and prick the bottom. Cover with a circle of greaseproof paper and fill with ceramic or dried beans and bake 'blind' in a pre-heated oven set at 425F/Gas Mark 7/220C for 10 minutes, then remove the beans and paper. Continue cooking for a further 10 minutes, or until it has begun to shrink slightly from the sides and has begun to brown lightly. Pour in the sauce, lay the salmon on top and decorate with the sliced egg. Spread with the crème fraîche and put in the oven for 5 minutes to heat through.

Steamed Salmon Pudding

In Norway, one of the Meccas of salmon fishermen, the locals make a delicious light pudding which counteracts the richness of the fish and makes an unusual hot main course for a summer dinner party.

—————————— *Serves 4 - 6* ——————————

1 lb (500g) filleted salmon
2 ½ tablespoons (35ml) potato flour
2 teaspoons fresh, chopped or 1 teaspoon dried, dill
salt and pepper
1½ pint (300ml) milk
¼ pint (150ml) single cream
butter
breadcrumbs

Skin the fish and chop roughly. Place in the food processor with the potato flour, herbs and seasonings and whizz until smooth, then gradually pour the milk and then the cream through the funnel. When it is all incorporated, tip into a 2½ pint (1.4 litre) oblong mould buttered and coated with breadcrumbs. Cover with buttered foil and cook in a water bath on top of the stove, or in a pre-heated oven at 400F/Gas Mark 6/200C for 45 minutes. Turn out very carefully and garnish with slices of lemon.

Serve with Hollandaise sauce, and new potatoes cooked in their skins and dressed with wine vinegar, olive oil, sugar and salt, and young broad beans tossed in butter and marjoram.

Marrow Chutney

Gone are the days when every cottage garden would have a profusion of gigantic marrows glowing in colours ranging from mottled green to cream and deepest orange. Many of these monsters were entered in the local flower show, but as a vegetable they had usually passed their 'sell by' date and the only thing to be done with them was to make them into chutney or, in some cases, rum. I never had any success with the latter, but country lore said that you should hang the marrow up in a net (old tights would do) cut off the top and remove seeds, then fill it with dark brown muscovado sugar. This would eventually drip through the uncut end into a bowl and the final result be bottled and drunk at Christmas time. To make the chutney this is what you do.
Makes 4 – 6 1lb (500g) pots.

3 lb (1.5kg) marrow, peeled and cut up
1½ lbs (750g) demerara sugar
2 level teaspoons salt
8 oz (250g) onions or shallots, peeled and cut up
8 oz (250g) cooking apples, peeled and cut up
8 oz (250g) sultanas
1½ pints (900ml) malt vinegar
1½ oz (15g) dried ginger ground ginger
2 teaspoons mixed pickling spice, tied in muslin

Put everything into a large preserving pan and cook slowly until thick and dark. Remove the bag of spices, pour into heated jars and cover. This goes particularly well with Salmon Kedgeree.

Sorrel Mayonnaise

This delicious relative of the common dock grows wild and can be found in old un-sprayed pasture and on hillsides. However, you need to be pretty dedicated to pick enough of the little arrow shaped leaves for any serious cooking. Luckily it is very easy to cultivate and will thrive in a window-box, large pot, or the border. I grow mine just outside the front door and find it enhances many things from salads to sauces and soups.

4 oz (125g) sorrel
4 oz (125g) cooked, chopped spinach
mayonnaise (see p.168)

Blanch the sorrel, chop finely, and add to the cooled, cooked spinach. Sorrel goes a rather unappealing colour so the spinach is there to make the sauce nice and green. Make the mayonnaise (see p.168), but don't put in the lemon juice or vinegar until you have added the sorrel and spinach as you may need less if the sauce tastes too sharp.

Nun's 'Puffs'

I could not resist including this pudding which originated over two hundred years ago at l'Abbaye de Baumes-les-Dames in France and was called *'Pets de Nonnes'*. They are a delicacy that are as light as air. The original recipe called for orange flower water, but I have adapted it by using rose geranium sugar, which I find adds a delicate flavour to lots of sweet things. To make this just put 2 or 3 rose geranium leaves in a jar of sugar, screw the top on tightly and leave for 2 weeks. Use as required.

———————— *Serves 4 - 6* ————————

1 pint (600ml) water
¼ teaspoon salt
4 oz (125g) butter
4 oz (125g) flour
4 eggs
1 tablespoon (15ml) rose geranium sugar or
  1 tablespoon (15ml) plain sugar and
  ½ teaspoon orange flower water
oil for frying

Heat up the water, salt and butter in a saucepan until it boils and then add the flour, stirring until it forms a dough. Remove from heat and beat in the eggs one at a time. Add rose geranium sugar, or sugar and orange flower water, last. Deep fry dessert-spoonfuls in hot fat. When they are brown remove and drain on kitchen paper.

Serve with a purée of apple, or rhubarb, flavoured with rose geranium sugar. (If using orange flower water to flavour the Nun's 'Puffs' use plain sugar, and cook the rhubarb or apple with orange peel.)

TROUT

My only claim to fame as a poacher happened on Exmoor when I was twelve. My parents used to take me down there for holidays, and the farmhouse where we stayed was owned by descendants of R.D. Blackmore, who wrote *Lorna Doone*. The two sons of the house were experts in the art of 'tickling trout' which they were kind enough to demonstrate to me. Fired with enthusiasm I decided to escape the grown-ups and have a go at it myself. I selected a likely rock and after what seemed like hours, imperceptibly slid my hand down under the belly of the resident trout, moving the water so that it caressed his tummy. Finally, taking a deep breath, I managed to seize the fish by sticking my finger and thumb in his gills and hoicked him out. With a certain amount of pride, and feeling that I was some sort of latter day Maid Marian, I was admiring my catch when, in the distance I spied the river keeper. The only place I could think of to secrete the fish was up my elasticated bloomers. It worked, and he passed by all unsuspecting. No fish that I have caught since has given me such pleasure.

I think my daughter Lucy felt the same thrill when she succeeded in hooking and landing a large trout by dangling a cigarette stub impaled on a hook over a weir. This method of catching a fish would have been considered peculiar anyway, but the fact that it took place within spitting distance of the keeper, on one of the better known beats of the River Test, where only fishing with a dry fly is allowed, made it an even greater feat.

Trout Fried with Bacon and Oatmeal

This method of cooking trout should really only be attempted with freshly caught wild brown trout. Scottish, Welsh or Irish burns or lochs are the last bastion of these gourmet delights. They are usually the more enjoyable for the hard work entailed in catching them. Perhaps a long, hard climb to some inaccessible loch twinkling like a jewel in the heather-clad hills, silent except for the cry of the curlew or the 'go-back, go-back' of the grouse, or a difficult walk across the rocks and boulders to a rushing, peaty-gold burn or the upper reaches of a river adds to the final enjoyment.

———————— *Serves 2* ————————

2 - 4 brown trout
oatmeal
butter or bacon fat
bacon

Clean the fish and fillet them if you like. Sprinkle liberally with oatmeal. Fry or grill the bacon and remove to a plate. Cook the fish, skin side down if frying and skin side up if grilling, until the skin is brown and coming up in bubbles. Then turn them over, sprinkle with more oatmeal and cook for a few minutes longer. They should be juicy inside and have a crisp coating of oatmeal.

Liberally buttered bread is the only accompaniment necessary, and if camping a hot, strong cup of tea with a 'slug' of whisky.

Trout with Bacon and Potatoes

This is an excellent way of disguising the often muddy taste of stillwater rainbow trout and it makes a good solid, no-nonsense supper dish. The recipe is of Austrian peasant origin and was given to me by one of our pigeon shooting friends who was a fanatical fisherman

—————————— *Serves 4 - 6* ——————————

1½ lbs (750g) trout, filleted
salt and pepper
juice of 1 lemon
2 oz (50g) butter
1 lb (500g) sliced cooked potatoes
4 oz (125g) smoked bacon rashers cut into bits
1 large onion, cut into rings
½ pint (300ml) sour cream or smetana
1 teaspoon paprika

Remove skin from the trout fillets and cut the flesh into chunks, sprinkle with salt and lemon juice and leave for 1 hour. Butter a 2 pint (1 litre) fireproof dish and half fill with potato slices. Lay the trout on top, and sprinkle with bacon and onion rings. Season with salt and pepper, pour over cream into which you have mixed the paprika, and cook in a pre-heated oven set at 400F/Gas Mark 6/200C for 20 - 30, minutes or until the top is browned. For a change, you can sprinkle with wholemeal bread-crumbs and grated cheese.

Lucy's Trout
with Coriander and Pink Peppercorns

Living in London, Lucy seldom comes by freshly caught trout so has to make do with the farmed trout she can buy in the supermarket. This is her way of dealing with the problem.

———————————— *Serves 2* ————————————

1 teaspoon coriander seeds
1 teaspoon pink peppercorns (usually obtainable in
*   supermarkets or delicatessen)*
2 tablespoons (30ml) hazelnut oil
2 oz (50g) ceps or porcini
salt and pepper
4 fillets of trout
1 bunch fresh parsley
oil for frying

Infuse the coriander seeds and pink peppercorns in hazelnut oil for 24 hours. Soak the ceps in warm water until soft, and then cook for 5 minutes in the soaking water. Drain, reserve liquid, and reduce by fast boiling. Chop ceps and mix with their juice. Spoon onto the filleted trout, season with salt and pepper, and fold each fillet over. Steam the trout for 10 minutes. Crush the coriander seeds and peppercorns, sprinkle over the cooked fish and garnish with crisply fried parsley.

Serve with new potatoes and french beans.

Smoked Trout Soufflé

This can either be made with the smoked trout, which you can buy in packets, or better still, the home smoked variety. If you do not have a proprietary trout smoker, it is not difficult to make one yourself. I have done it with an old stainless steel colander which held the lighted barbecue charcoal. This was then covered with a layer of sawdust (obtainable from any fishing tackle shop) and the fish laid on a grilling grid. The smoke was contained by a cardboard carton with the bottom half of one side cut out, but be careful not to set it alight. The other method is with a biscuit tin (see p.151).

─────────── *Serves 2* ───────────

4 smoked trout fillets, weighing approximately
   12 oz (350g)
¼ pint (150ml) milk
2 teaspoons cornflour
2 tablespoons (30ml) double cream
2 egg yolks
2 teaspoons parsley, chopped
1 teaspoon horseradish sauce
salt and pepper
3 egg whites, stiffly beaten
wholemeal breadcrumbs

Skin the trout fillets and whizz in a food processor, or mash with a fork. Put in a saucepan with the milk, add the cornflour mixed with a little water, and heat until thick, stirring constantly. Mix in the cream, egg yolks, parsley and seasoning, and finally fold in the egg whites. Spoon into a 7" (15cm) soufflé dish, sprinkle some wholemeal breadcrumbs on top, and place in a pre-heated oven at 400F/Gas Mark 6/200C for 20 - 30 minutes.

   Serve immediately.

Trout in Red Wine Jelly

This is a good way of using up that large rainbow trout lurking in your deep freeze and it makes a good centrepiece for a buffet.

——————————— *Serves 6 - 8* ———————————

1 rainbow trout weighing 2 - 3lb (900g - 1.4kg)
court bouillon (see p.161) using red instead of
*   white wine*
0.04 oz (25g) gelatine (see p.163)
salt and pepper
1 tablespoon (15ml) red wine vinegar
lemon slices

Place the cleaned trout in a fish kettle, pour over the cold court bouillon and cover. Bring slowly to the boil and simmer gently for 30 minutes, then leave to cool in the stock. Remove fish very carefully to a dish, skin, cover with cling film, and refrigerate. Clarify the stock (see p.162) and add the gelatine dissolved in the red wine vinegar (see p.163). Allow to cool to a syrupy consistency and then spoon carefully over the fish until it is completely coated. Transfer to a serving dish, garnish with lemon slices, and surround with the rest of the jellied stock, chopped.

Trout Pancakes

This a good way of using up left-over cooked or smoked trout. It makes an excellent supper dish or, if you make the pancakes small, it is a good 'starter'.

—————————— *Serves 4 - 6* ——————————

8 - 12 oz (250 - 350g) cooked trout
1½ pint (300ml) béchamel sauce (see p.166)
1 tablespoon (15ml) cream cheese
¼ pint (150ml) single cream)
1 oz (25g) grated Parmesan cheese
1 pinch cayenne pepper
salt and pepper
breadcrumbs
butter

Pancake Batter

4 oz (100g) plain flour
2 eggs
1 tablespoon (15ml) sunflower oil
½ pint (300ml) milk, approximately

Remove any bones from the trout and mix with the béchamel sauce (see p.166) and cream cheese. Make 8 pancakes. Put a spoonful of trout mixture on each one and roll up. Lay side by side in a shallow, oiled, 2 pint (1 litre) fireproof dish, pour over the cream, mixed with the cheese, cayenne pepper and seasoning to taste. Sprinkle with breadcrumbs and dot with butter. Place in a pre-heated oven set at 375F/Gas Mark 5/190C for 10 – 15 minutes. Serve with new potatoes and french beans.

As a starter, spread the trout mixture onto smaller pancakes and fold in three, arrange on a fireproof dish, dribble the cream and Parmesan down the centre and flash under a hot grill for a few seconds until it is brown and bubbling.

Elderflower Fritters

On a summer's evening as you wander along the grassy banks of a chalk stream your senses will be stunned by the heady scent of an elderflower bush, its creamy mass luminous in the failing light. Do take some heads home with you and make this delicious and delicate sweet. Of course you don't have to be a fisherman, as they grow in profusion along footpaths or even, possibly unwanted, at the bottom of your garden.

──────── *Serves 2- 4* ────────

8 - 12 elderflower heads
4 oz (125g) plain flour
2 eggs
¼ pint (150ml) beer or milk
1 tablespoon (15ml) sunflower oil
sunflower oil for frying
caster sugar
1 lemon

Make a thick batter from the flour, eggs and beer. Dip the flower heads in it and fry in deep, hot, oil until puffy and crisp. Dust with caster sugar and serve with lemon quarters.

Elderflower Champagne

Absolutely no apologies to the French champagne houses. As far as I am concerned it has always been known as Elderflower Champagne, and the old lady from whom I got the recipe would not have called it anything else. It is a non-alcoholic and refreshing drink, but, unlike other homemade beverages, it does not keep.

Makes approximately 6 x 1 pint (600ml) bottles.

6 heads of elderflower, or more if you wish
1 gallon (3.5 litres) water
1½ lbs (750g) sugar
2 tablespoons (15ml) cider vinegar
1 lemon, thinly peeled, rind and juice
Campden tablets

Steep the flower heads in the water in a large bowl with the sugar, juice and thinly peeled rind of the lemon for 2 days. Sterilize 6 – 8 screw-topped bottles with Campden tablets. Strain the elderflower mixture and pour into the bottles. Screw the tops on tightly and secure them with garden wire so that they don't explode. After 10 days, take the wire off and unscrew very slightly each day. It should be ready to drink in two weeks.

PIKE AND CARP

Some years ago I decided to try my hand at cooking pike, but the main obstacle was 'first catch your pike', so whilst Archie was fishing for salmon I set about trying to do.so. I attached all manner of bait to my rod but not even a 'Toby' nor, when that failed, a 'Mepps' succeeded in changing my luck. Fortunately one of the fishing tenants had caught a pike that morning, so the day was saved. In my conversation with him I discovered that he had got two the previous week and, not realising how good they were to eat, he had dropped them off at the local kennels for the hounds! When pike is mentoned, all people seem to say is "Oh! I supose you are going to make them into *quenelles de brochet*," this being the only recipe for pike they have heard about. In Europe and Russia things are different and there is a host of recipes attesting to their culinary worth.

Pike with Hot Horseradish Sauce

This is an Austro-Hungarian recipe which is very delicious, but serve the sauce separately as it is rather hot.

————————— Serves 4 - 6 —————————
1 pike weighing 4 lb (1.8kg)
court bouillon (see p.161)

Clean and decapitate the pike and immerse in the cold court bouillon. Bring to the boil and simmer, covered, for 30 minutes. Remove the fish, take off the skin, carefully ease off the fillets and arrange them on a serving dish. Cover with foil and keep warm whilst you make the sauce.

Hot Horseradish Sauce

3 oz (75g) butter
2 oz (50g) flour
½ pint (300ml) court bouillon (see p.161)
1 tablespoon (15ml) grated horseradish
1 heaped teaspoon paprika
salt and pepper
¼ pint (150ml) sour cream

For the sauce, melt the butter and add the flour, cook for a few minutes and then add the court bouillon and stir until smooth. Add the horseradish, paprika, salt and pepper, and simmer very gently, stirring occasionally so that it does not stick. Add the cream at the last minute but do not allow to boil. Remove foil from fish and pour the sauce over it, or serve separately.

Garnish with new potatoes sprinkled with plenty of parsley and serve with hot, diced, beetroot. This goes well with the sauce and makes a good colour contrast.

Baked Fillets of Pike with Cider

The original recipe, which was given to me by a French friend, used a dry, white Sancerre, but I think cider is just as nice, if not nicer.

―――――――― *Serves 4* ――――――――

1 pike, weighing approximately 3 lbs (1.4kg)
4 oz (125g) butter
5 - 6 shallots, peeled and finely chopped
1 pint (600ml) cider or Sancerre
salt and pepper
8 large mushrooms, peeled and chopped
juice of ½ lemon
½ pint (300ml) single cream

Clean and 'behead' the pike, and with a sharp knife remove and skin the fillets. Butter a 2 pint (1 litre) gratin dish lavishly, and sprinkle in the chopped shallots. Lay the fillets on top, and pour over your chosen liquid. Season with salt and pepper. Cook in a pre-heated oven set at 350F/Gas Mark 4/175C for 30 minutes or until done, basting frequently. Remove pike fillets to a serving dish, cover with foil and keep warm. Cook the mushrooms in a little butter and the lemon juice, add to the liquid the fish was cooked in and reduce to half by fast boiling. Add the cream and cook for a few seconds longer. Whizz in the food processor and pour over the fish.

Decorate with slices of lemon and surround with a border of rice. Serve with a salad of lambs lettuce and rocket dressed with hazelnut oil and lemon juice.

Russian Stuffed Pike

When I went to Russia this is one of the dishes I ate and I immediately knew it would appeal to my family as it is boneless. It is quite a fiddle to skin but worth it in the end for the accolades you will receive.

─────────── *Serves 4 - 6* ───────────

1 pike weighing 3½ lbs (1.5kg)
4 oz (125g) white bread, crusts removed
1 onion, peeled and roughly chopped
¼ pint (150ml) milk
2 oz (50g) butter, softened
1 pinch grated nutmeg
salt and pepper
4 pints (1.8 litres) court bouillon (see p.161)

Run a sharp knife round the pike just below the head and gills and try to pull the skin off intact, like a glove. Detach any difficult bits by easing under the skin with the knife. Remove the flesh and put into the food processor with the bread, onion, milk, butter and seasonings. Blend until smooth, adding a little extra water if necessary. Fill the skin and sew up the openings. Wrap in foil and lower into the cold court-bouillon (see p.161). Bring slowly to the boil, poach very gently for 30 minutes and allow the pike to get completely cold in the liquid. Lift out very gently and cut into slices. Lay these on a dish and garnish with slices of lemon and sweet pickled gherkin.

Serve with a Russian salad of diced cold cooked carrots, peas, potatoes, french beans, beetroot and cucumber. Season with a little oil and vinegar, salt and pepper and, just before serving, turn the salad in half mayonnaise and half sour cream. Serve a homemade mayonnaise (see p.168) to which you have added a chopped hard-boiled egg, some capers and some anchovies.

147

Stuffed Carp

Carp is much esteemed in Europe and also in China. It is wise to get someone to clean and de-scale the carp for you. If you have to do it yourself, it helps to bend the fish in a semi circle so that the scales are protruding, which makes it easier to scrape them off. In Germany it is traditional to eat carp on Christmas Eve, but on this occasion the scales are left on so that each guest can take one home as a good luck charm for the rest of the year.

—————————— *Serves 4 - 6* ——————————

1 carp, approximately 2 lbs (1 kg)
1 slice stale bread, made into crumbs
1 hard-boiled egg, chopped,
1 oz (25g) sorrel, chopped
2 shallots, peeled and finely chopped
2 oz (50g) butter, melted
salt and pepper

Mix together the stuffing ingredients and spoon them into the fish's stomach cavity. Wrap the carp in well-buttered foil and bake in a pre-heated oven at 350F/Gas Mark 4/175C for 20 - 30 minutes, or until done.

Serve with spinach and buttered noodles.

Easy Wild Plum Ice Cream

This is the easiest ice cream to make as you don't need an ice cream maker and you don't have to keep remembering to stir the mixture every 30 minutes. Wild plums are wonderful if you can find them growing in an old hedge but Victoria plums or damsons will do just as well, or indeed any fruit.

─────────── *Serves 6 - 8* ───────────

1 lb (500g) wild plums
1 tablespoon (15ml) lemon juice
3 egg yolks
¼ pint (150ml) Greek yoghurt
½ pint (300ml) double cream, whipped to
   soft peaks
3 egg whites
6 oz (175g) caster sugar

Cook the plums with 1 tablespoon (15ml) of water until soft, and then remove the stones. Heat through, and place in the food processor with the lemon juice. Switch on and add the egg yolks through the funnel one by one. Tip the purée into a bowl and when cool stir in the yoghurt and then fold in the whipped cream. Beat the egg whites stiffly, and add the sugar in 3 lots and continue beating until it is stiff and shiny. Fold into the plum purée and spoon into a straight-sided 2 pint (1 litre) soufflé dish and place in the freezer. Take out 1 hour before it is to be eaten and put in the fridge. If you forget, all is not lost; just take it out and leave at room temperature while you are having your drinks, and it should be ready to eat when you get to the pudding course.

EEL

Eel is a much underrated fish, and for those who in times past lived near a river would have been a marvellous source of food. In Holland eel is highly thought of and can be found on most restaurant menus. I sampled some on a visit to a friend in the month of July. We sailed to an island which is part of his shoot and, as we disembarked, a waft of smoke reached us. By the water's edge stood a homemade smoker tended by the old keeper who, that morning, had caught dozens of eels in his traps. Several beers and Hollands gins later, the eels were pronounced to be done and were handed round. No such niceties as plates, knives and forks! Skinning was achieved by hand, and teeth nibbled the sweet, succulent and smoky flesh from the bones. Accompanied by fresh bread with farm butter and cheese, it was truly a meal fit for the Gods. Eel Pie and Mash and Jellied Eel still survive in one or two places in London, but if you can, get hold of eel from your fishmonger, or maybe catch one or two, or bribe a river keeper to let you have some from his traps as there are some very good recipes.

Eel Pâté

This is best made with eels that have been smoked in a trout smoker (a hot smoker). If you do not have such a smoker you can improvise. A biscuit tin placed on two bricks will be quite adequate. Cover the base of the tin with 4 tablespoons (60ml) of smoking sawdust from a fishing tackle shop. Crumple up some wire netting into the tin and stand an enamel plate or metal container on it to catch the drips. Spread some more netting or a grill grid (if it will fit inside the tin) over the plate, lay your eels on top and sprinkle with salt. Put the lid on the biscuit tin and stand it on two bricks. Fill a small tin, such as the bottom of a tobacco or boiled sweet tin, with methylated spirits. Slide underneath the biscuit tin and light. When it goes out your eels will be smoked. Remove with care, and try not to spill the juice from the plate. You can also smoke trout in this contraption.

———— Serves 4 - 6 ————

8 oz (300g) smoked eel, skinned and boned
2 oz (50g) butter, softened
1 teaspoon creamed horseradish
1 tablespoon (15ml) fromage frais
juice drippings
lemon juice to taste
2 teaspoons chopped parsley
salt and freshly ground black pepper

Place everything in a blender or food processor and whizz until smooth. Otherwise mix together in a bowl with a fork. The amount of butter depends on how much eel there is. You just have to judge the amounts and keep tasting. I like to add fromage frais, as eel is very rich, but you can replace it with cream if you wish.

Serve with pumpernickel, rye or crisp bread.

Eel in Green Herb Sauce

This recipe uses country ingredients, including nettle tops in season, so don't forget your gloves when you pick them!

————————— Serves 2 - 4 —————————

4 small to medium eels, skinned and cut into
 2" (5cm) chunks
butter for frying
1 shallot, peeled and finely chopped
1 stalk celery, scraped and finely diced
white wine or dry cider
2 oz (50g) each sorrel, watercress, and nettle tops,
 roughly chopped
1 tablespoon (15ml) each parsley and chervil,
 chopped
salt and pepper

Fry the chunks of eel in the butter with the shallots and celery, then moisten with a little wine or cider and throw in the herbs and cook for a few seconds or until they have wilted. Season with salt and pepper.

Serve with George Parker's mashed potato, and carrot and watercress purée.

George Parker's Mashed Potato

Peel some old potatoes, preferably Desirée or a similar floury variety. When they are cooked, drain well, cover with 3 or 4 thicknesses of greaseproof paper, a tea towel and saucepan lid. Stand on a very, very low heat or at the side of the Aga for 30 minutes, add plenty of salt and pepper and masses of butter and mash well. It may seem a long-winded way of making mashed potatoes, but it is really worth the trouble.

Mary's Lemon Cheesecake

Until I ate this cheesecake, made by my daughter Lucy's sister-in-law, I had not much liked cheesecakes, but this one converted me into an addict.

Serves 4 – 6

Case

11-12 digestive biscuits, crumbled
2 oz (50g) soft brown sugar
2 oz (50g) butter, melted

Filling

4 oz (125g) cottage cheese
1½ lemons, grated rind and squeezed juice
2 oz (50g) caster sugar
4 oz (125g) Philadelphia cream cheese
0.4 oz (11g) gelatine (see p.163)
¼ pint of whipping cream
2 egg whites

For the case, mix together the biscuit crumbs and sugar, stir in the melted butter and line the base and sides of a loose based 8" (20cm) flan tin, pressing it down firmly. Chill until needed. For the filling, beat the cottage cheese and lemon rind until completely smooth, or whizz in a food processor. Add caster sugar and Philadelphia cream cheese and beat or whizz again. Dissolve the gelatine in the lemon juice and add slowly to the mixture whilst still beating. Turn into a large bowl. Whip the cream and the egg whites seperately to soft peaks and fold first the cream and then the egg whites gently into the cheese mixture. Pour into the lined flan dish and chill for at least two hours, or freeze until needed.

CRAYFISH

When we first came to live in Hampshire, friends of ours had a stretch of chalk stream, and from early August crayfishing parties were held. The crayfish were hauled out in their homemade traps which had previously been baited with pieces of kipper. A camp fire was built and the crayfish were plunged into boiling, salted water, cooked, and eaten in the fingers with thick slices of bread and butter and copious swigs of alcohol. At that time there were professional crayfishermen, and one in particular used to fish the River Test. His method, though somewhat unappealing, was most successful. He used to collect beasts heads from the abattoir and chuck them into the river. He would come back later, pull them out, and remove a goodly harvest of crayfish. My publisher tells me that on a boating holiday with his family in France, his daughter dived into the river and when she emerged there was a crayfish locked onto her long hair! Sadly, our indigenous crayfish has become scarce due to pollution, but farmed crayfish should be obtainable from good fishmongers.

Crayfish, Swedish Style

The Swedes are very keen on crayfish and often hold crayfishing parties by the light of the August moon, with trees hung with paper lanterns. This recipe caters for live crayfish. It is advisable, just before cooking, to remove the intestinal tube or the crayfish will taste bitter. To do this, kill the crayfish by plunging a knife through the carapace (or hard shell) just behind the head, then remove the intestinal tube from beneath the opening under the middle section of the tail.

——————— *Serves 4 - 6* ———————

30 crayfish
6 pints (2.5 litres) boiling water
5 tablespoons (75ml) sea salt
10 - 12 sprigs fresh dill

Plunge the crayfish, ten at a time, into the boiling, salted water, with a handful of dill, cover and cook for 6 - 7 minutes. Scoop out, bring water back to the boil, and continue until all the crayfish are cooked. Add more dill, cool, and refrigerate. Arrange on a platter and serve with toast and butter or wholemeal bread.

Crayfish can also be cooked in white wine and shallots, shelled, tossed in butter and flamed in brandy. The shells and claws can be used to make a good soup.

Wholemeal Bread

After the corn had been cut and the binder had been round tying it into sheaves, it was all hands on deck to stack them into stooks to dry. Many village women and children did this back-breaking job, which I remember doing myself during the war. One of the perks was that you were allowed to take home the 'gleanings' for your hens, ducks, or whatever. Frankie, my daughter's nanny, told us that she used to glean by the light of the moon. This recipe is fatal for anyone on a diet as the smell of the newly baked bread makes you want to go on eating it forever.

Makes 2 large, or 4 small loaves.

3 lbs (1.5kg) wholemeal flour
2 level teaspoons salt
2 level tablespoons (60ml) sugar
1 oz (25g) lard
1 teaspoon sugar, dissolved in 1½ pints (900ml)
   warm water
2 level tablespoons (30ml) dried yeast

Mix the dry ingredients. Stir the dried yeast into the sugar and water and leave until bubbles form. Mix together and work to a firm dough. Turn out onto a floured surface and knead and stretch for 10 minutes (or mix half quantities in a food mixer with a dough hook). Place the dough in a greased mixing bowl and cover with a clean tea towel. Leave for 1 hour in a warm place, such as an airing cupboard or by an Aga, longer if the temperature is not so warm. The dough should have doubled in size. 'Knock back' by flattening with the knuckles, turn out onto a floured surface and knead as before. Divide into two oblong 2 lb (1 kg) greased tins or lay on a greased baking sheet. Cover with a tea towel and leave to rise in a warm place as before, to double the size. Pre-heat the oven to 450F/Gas Mark 8/230C and bake on the centre shelf for 30 - 40, minutes or longer if necessary. The loaves should have shrunken slightly from the sides of the tin and sound hollow when tapped underneath.

Wild Strawberry Shortcake

For many years, Archie and I grew cultivated wild strawberries, or *Fraises des Bois,* commercially. We had 1½ acres of them. If you cannot find enough to make this pudding, you will just have to make do with ordinary strawberries.

—————————— *Serves 6 - 8* ——————————

6 oz (175g) plain flour
1 pinch salt
4 oz (125g) butter
3 oz (75g) ground almonds
3 oz (80g) caster sugar
1 egg yolk

Strawberry Filling

8 oz (250g) wild or cultivated
   strawberries
2 oz (50g) sugar
1 egg white
lemon juice
¼ pint (150ml) crème fraîche

Sift together the flour and salt, and tip into the food processor. Add the butter, cut into little pieces, and whizz for 15 seconds. Add the ground almonds and sugar and the egg yolk. Switch on, and process until it has cohered. Divide into two and roll out to ½" (1cm). Cut into 2 circles 6" (15cm) in diameter, and place on a greased baking sheet. Prick with a fork and cook in a pre-heated oven set at 325F/Gas Mark 3/160C for 30 minutes. Cool slightly, and transfer to a wire tray. Hull the strawberries and sprinkle with half the sugar and a little lemon juice. Whisk the egg white until stiff, add the remaining sugar, and continue beating until it is thick. Beat the crème fraîche and fold it into the egg white. If using wild strawberries leave them whole, otherwise cut them into pieces and fold into the egg white mixture. Spread the mixture over one round of pastry and place the other one on top. Sprinkle with caster sugar and serve immediately.

BASIC RECIPES

These are some of the most frequently recurring basic recipes which I have collected together in one chapter. This avoids long and unwieldy descriptions in the individual recipes and, is mainly for those who are not quite such experienced cooks.

Basic Cooked Marinade

This can be used for venison, hare or wild boar. You can play about with it and add other spices, orange or lemon peel or whatever takes your fancy.

1 Spanish onion, peeled and chopped
2 carrots, peeled and chopped
2 cloves garlic, peeled and chopped
2 tablespoons (30ml) best olive oil
1 bottle Burgundy or red wine
1 tablespoon (15ml) dark brown muscovado sugar
10 black peppercorns
6 juniper berries
3 whole cloves
2 tablespoons (30ml) red wine vinegar
sprigs of rosemary, thyme, parsley, bay leaf

'Sweat' the vegetables in the oil over a low heat, then pour in the burgundy, add the sugar, peppercorns, juniper berries, cloves and vinegar and simmer for 20 minutes. Leave until absolutely cold, and then pour over your chosen joint, strew with the herbs, cover loosely with foil and leave in a cool place or the bottom of the fridge for 2 days, turning morning and evening.

Game Forcemeat

This is a general recipe for forcemeat. You can alter it according to the game you are cooking. For particular species add the livers sautéed and vary the seasoning according to your whim.
   Makes 18 forcemeat balls.

> *3 oz (75g) fresh breadcrumbs*
> *1 oz (25g) butter*
> *1 teaspoon each, chopped parsley, marjoram,*
>   *thyme, grated lemon rind*
> *1 rasher bacon, de-rinded, chopped and fried*
> *game livers trimmed and sautéed in butter,*
>   *chopped finely or whizzed in the food processor*
>   *for a few seconds*
> *1 egg, beaten*
> *2 tablespoons (30ml) milk*
> *1 pinch cayenne pepper*
> *salt and pepper*

If the game livers are on the meagre side you can bulk them up by using a couple of trimmed chicken livers. Mix together all the ingredients. Scoop out with a teaspoon and form into balls. Either fry in hot fat for 10 minutes, or bake in a pre-heated oven set at 400F/Gas Mark 6/200C for 15 - 20 minutes.

Rich Brown Game Stock

If you are using venison bones try and chop or saw them up into
4" (10cm) pieces. It is not essential but does make for a better
flavoured stock.

2 tablespoons (30ml) olive oil
1 onion, peeled and chopped
2 carrots, peeled and chopped
1 leek, trimmed and cut into 1" (2cm) pieces
1 stalk celery, chopped
game bones
1 pig's trotter, split (optional)
1 sprig each thyme, marjoram, parsley
1 bay leaf
6 peppercorns
6 juniper berries
3 pints (1.8 litres) water

Switch the oven on and set at 450F/Gas Mark 8/230C. Heat the
oil in a roasting tin on top of the stove and brown the vegetables
and bones, then transfer to the oven and roast for 30 minutes.
Remove and pour in the water, stir round well to incorporate
any brown bits and transfer to a saucepan. Add the rest of the
ingredients, cover and bring to the boil. Simmer for 1 - 1½ hours,
skimming periodically, then strain through a colander. Blot off
any fat with squares of kitchen paper. If not intended for
immediate use I cool it and then pour it into washed out milk
cartons, label and freeze it. If the recipe requires reduced stock,
boil it rapidly until it begins to look syrupy and tastes concentrated. Salt should only be added at the end of cooking. If using
a pig's trotter, gelatine will not be necessary to set the stock for
use in any cold dish.

White Game Stock

This is the kind of stock I normally make where the recipe does not call for a rich stock. It is suitable for stews, sauces, and as a liquid in which to stew game. Use all the ingredients listed in Rich Brown Game Stock (above) except the olive oil. Place in a large saucepan, bring to the boil and simmer gently for 1½ – 2 hours. If I am in a hurry and have, for example, one pheasant carcass I put it into a 5 pint (2 litre) oven-proof glass mixing bowl, cover with a plate, place in the microwave and switch it on to high for 1 hour.

Court Bouillon

Court bouillon when translated means 'short boiling'. It is a flavoured liquid used for poaching fish, game or poultry, where a delicate flavour is required. It is also the cook's answer when she hasn't got stock and has run out of stock cubes!

3 onions and 3 shallots, peeled
2 cloves garlic, peeled (optional)
1 leek, cleaned and trimmed
1 carrot, scraped
2 bay leaves
1 sprig each thyme and parsley
1/2 pint (300ml) white wine
4 pints (2.3 litres) water
1 tablespoon (15ml) white wine vinegar
salt and pepper

Bring all the ingredients slowly to the boil and simmer, uncovered, for 30 minutes. Allow to cool before use, unless recipe states otherwise. Strain when cold.

Fish Stock or Fumet

Roughly translated, *fumet* means flavour, of meat or fish. It is, therefore, the fishy equivalent to concentrated or rich game stock.

> *1oz (25g) butter*
> *fish trimmings from your fishmonger, if you can*
> * get them (or save heads, bones and skin when*
> * you have a filleting session and freeze them)*
> *1 carrot, onion, leek, stick celery, peeled, cleaned*
> * and trimmed*
> *2 bay leaves*
> *1 sprig each parsley, thyme, marjoram and*
> * tarragon (or a sachet of bouquet garni)*
> *4 white peppercorns*
> *1 pint (600ml) white wine*
> *1 pint (600ml) water*
> *½ teaspoon salt*

Melt the butter in a saucepan, add the fish bones, vegetables, herbs and peppercorns, then cover and cook over a very gentle heat for 15 minutes. Shake the pan every so often, and make sure the contents do not brown. Add the wine, water and salt, and simmer gently for 30 minutes. Cool and strain.

Clarifying Stock

This is not so difficult as it sounds, and is worth the trouble when you see the crystal clear liquid.

> *1½ pints (900ml) strained stock*
> *2 egg whites, plus shells*

Beat the egg whites up with one third of the stock in a 4 pint (2.3 litre) saucepan until frothy. Add the crunched-up egg shells, and pour on the rest of the stock in a thin stream, whisking constantly. Place the saucepan over a moderate heat with the handle facing you and agitate gently with a wire whisk until it begins to simmer.

Leave to 'shiver' for 15 minutes without stirring, then give the handle a quarter turn to the left and repeat this process every 15 minutes until you have completed the circle. Lay a clean, scalded tea towel over a colander and carefully ladle the stock into it and let it drain. You should now have a sparkling liquid.

Gelatine and Aspic

For some reason the use of gelatine or aspic gives some people the 'heebie jeebies'. It is not really difficult if you remember that the liquid used to dissolve gelatine must on no account boil. Aspic, on the other hand, must be sprinkled into fast boiling liquid.

Gelatine Granules

1 x 0.04 oz (11g) sachet sets 1 pint (600ml) liquid

METHOD 1: Have a jug or bowl of 1 - 2 tablespoons (15 - 30ml) hot *but not boiling* water, sprinkle the gelatine granules over it and stir until dissolved. If using lemon juice or other liquid, first sprinkle in the granules and place the bowl or jug in a saucepan of warm water. Heat gently and stir until dissolved.

METHOD 2: Tip the gelatine into a glass measuring jug, then pour in 2 tablespoons (30ml) water and let it sit for a few minutes until it looks spongy. Put in the microwave and switch on at high for 30 seconds. If the weather is very hot and thundery you may need to use an extra teaspoon of gelatine to get a 'set'. Stir well when you take it out to make sure it has all dissolved.

Leaf Gelatine

This is used by all top class chefs but is less readily available, though you can find it in some delicatessen and specialist shops.

1 leaf = approximately 0.04 oz (11g)
and sets 1 pint (600ml) liquid

Soak the leaf in cold water for a few minutes and add to the hot liquid. Stir until dissolved.

Aspic

1 oz (25g) aspic granules sets 1 pint (600ml) liquid

Bring ¼ pint (150ml) water to the boil, sprinkle in the granules and stir until dissolved. Make up the quantity with cold water.

Hot Water Crust

12 oz (350g) plain flour
1 teaspoon salt
4 oz (125g) lard
1/4 pint (150ml) water
1 egg, beaten

Sift together the flour and salt into a bowl and stand in a warm place. Melt the lard in a saucepan, add the water and bring to the boil. Make a well in the flour, pour in the lard and water and mix well with a wooden spoon. Turn onto a lightly floured surface and knead until smooth. Form quickly into the shape required as if this pastry is left to get cool it will become difficult to handle. Cover and keep warm any pastry you are not using, for example any that you have set aside for a lid.

Shortcrust Pastry

The fat used for this type of pastry is very much a question of personal preference. I use concentrated cooking butter, when available, or plain butter if not. Some people prefer to use margarine or a mixture of butter and lard, or all lard. Lard alone produces a very short crumbly pastry and was nearly always used by cottagers, as lard from the pig would have been the only fat readily available.

6 oz (75g) plain flour
1 teaspoon icing sugar (for sweet pies)
1 pinch salt
4 oz (125g) butter
2 tablespoons (30ml) cold water

Sift the flour, sugar and salt into a bowl. Drop in the butter cut into small pieces and rub it into the flour mixture with your fingertips until it resembles fine breadcrumbs. Add the water and mix in with a knife, adding a drop or two more if the mixture looks too dry. Form into a ball, sprinkle with flour and wrap in cling film. Refrigerate for 30 minutes before rolling out. If you have a food processor, sieve the dry ingredients into the processor bowl, and drop in the butter pieces. Switch on and process for 15 seconds then pour the liquid through the funnel until it amalgamates into a ball.

Cobbler Topping

This is a scone type topping which is used instead of pastry for covering pies.

Sweet Cobbler Topping

4 oz (125g) self raising flour
1 pinch salt
1 teaspoon sugar
1 oz (25g) butter
3 tablespoons (45ml) milk, approximately

Sieve the flour, salt and sugar into a bowl or food processor bowl. Rub in the butter, and mix in the milk until you have a soft dough. Roll out ½" (1cm) thick and cut into 2" (5cm) rounds. Lay in overlapping rows on top of the chosen pie filling and cook in a pre-heated oven set at 400F/Gas Mark 6/200C for 20 - 30 minutes, or until golden brown.

Cheese Cobbler Topping

4 oz (125g) self-raising flour
1 pinch salt
1 pinch cayenne pepper
1 oz (25g) butter
1 oz (25g) mature Cheddar cheese, grated
3 tablespoons (60ml) milk, approximately

Sieve the flour, salt and cayenne pepper into a bowl or food processor bowl. Rub in the butter, mix in the grated cheese, and add enough milk to make a soft dough. Turn onto a floured surface and roll out to ½" (1cm) thick. Cut into 2" (5cm) rounds and lay in overlapping rows on top of the chosen meat filling. Cook in a pre-heated oven set at 400F/Gas Mark 6/200C for 20 - 30 minutes or until golden brown. If liked a little extra grated cheese can be sprinkled over the topping before it goes in the oven.

Béchamel Sauce

This is the basis of all kinds of sauces and is not difficult to make. Always use plain flour as lumps are more likely to form with self-raising flour.

1 onion slice
1 bay leaf
6 peppercorns
1 pint (600ml) milk
2 oz (50g) butter
2 oz (50g) plain flour
salt and pepper

Infuse the onion slice, bay leaf and peppercorns in the milk over a low heat but do not allow to boil. Strain. Melt the butter in a saucepan, add the flour and cook over a low heat for 2 minutes, stirring constantly. Remove from heat and pour in all the milk, whisking continuously with a wire whisk as you do so. When it is all amalgamated return to the stove and bring slowly to the boil stirring with a wooden spoon until it thickens. Simmer for 5 minutes, but whisk or stir to prevent the sauce burning or sticking to the saucepan. If disaster strikes and it is lumpy, all is not lost. Either pass through a sieve, process in a food processor or blender, or get the lumps out with one of those magical hand-held electric mixers. A thinner sauce can be obtained by adding more liquid until the right consistency is obtained. If you want a real velouté sauce, allow it to simmer over the lowest possible heat for 1 hour. Any kind of liquid can be used to make the sauce, for instance a rich brown stock will give you a brown sauce and white stock can be used as part of the liquid for the sauce for a fricassée.

Beurre Manié

Beurre manié can be used when you wish to thicken a stew or casserole. It consists of equal quantities of flour and butter kneaded together. The resultant mixture is then dropped into the boiling liquid in tiny bits and whisked until it is amalgamated and the right thickness is obtained.

1 oz (25g) plain flour
1 oz (25g) butter, softened to room temperature

The easiest way to make the beurre manié is to knead it in a bowl with the back of a spoon or with a fork. 1 oz (25g) will thicken approximately 1 pint (600ml) liquid, but it is really a question of dropping in little bits until it looks right. I usually make quite a quantity, chill it in the fridge, cut it in bits and freeze it on to cling film on a baking tray. I then transfer it to a plastic bag, and it is ready for use when required.

Mayonnaise

As easy as falling off a log, if you know how. It really is not at all difficult and even when made with a fork doesn't take as long as you would imagine.
Makes ½ pint (300ml).

2 egg yolks
1 level teaspoon mild Dijon mustard
½ pint (300ml) sunflower oil
2 teaspoons white wine vinegar
1 good pinch sugar
salt and pepper

Put the egg yolks and mustard into a bowl and beat with a fork, wire whisk, or electric beaters. Whilst doing this pour the oil in drop by drop to begin with and then, when the mixture begins to thicken, in a steady trickle. Finally, beat in the vinegar, sugar, salt and pepper. A few drops of boiling water will prevent it from going oily when you put it in the fridge. It is best not to use very new laid eggs, and be sure to take them out of the fridge at least 1 hour before using so that they are at the same temperature as the oil.

Blender Mayonnaise

This is made with one whole egg instead of 2 egg yolks. The rest of the ingredients are the same. Put the egg in the blender, or food processor, with the mustard and switch on. Whilst it is whizzing pour the oil slowly through the funnel, as in the previous recipe, and finally the rest of the ingredients. This is creamier and not quite so rich. I prefer it as a dressing for potato salad.

Hollandaise Sauce

As with mayonnaise this is not half as difficult as it sounds. Just think of it as warm mayonnaise made with melted butter instead of oil.

3 - 4 egg yolks
2 teaspoons white wine
2 teaspoons water
2 teaspoons lemon juice
4 - 6 oz (125 - 175g) unsalted butter,
  cut into dice
ice cubes (optional)
salt and pepper

Put the egg yolks, wine, water and lemon juice into a bowl. If you don't have any wine use 1 tablespoon (15ml) water instead. Sit the bowl over a saucepan of hot, but not boiling, water and whisk in the butter bit by bit until the sauce thickens. Season and pour into a warm, but not hot, sauceboat and serve immediately. If it looks like curdling or separating add an ice cube and remove the bowl from the saucepan.

Blender Hollandaise Sauce

Melt the butter. Warm the goblet or bowl of your blender or food processor. Tip in the egg yolks, switch on, and pour the melted butter slowly through the funnel. When it has thickened add the wine, water, lemon juice, salt and pepper.

INDEX